CONTENTS

Abbreviations 2
Acknowledgements. 2

1 Introduction 2
2 Eden Wants Action 4
3 British Military Planning 6
4 Resources Available 9
5 Training 14
6 Deployment from the UK 19
7 Slide towards Musketeer 24
8 31 October: Evening, the War Starts 29
9 Crews: Downtime on Base Between Raids 42
10 1 November: Evening Raids 44
11 'Phase 1...has been achieved' 48
12 Raids of 3 November 54
13 Raids of 5 November 58
14 6 November: Ceasefire 60
15 Commentary and Assessments 62

Bibliography 67
Notes 68
About the Author 72

Helion & Company Limited
Unit 8 Amherst Business Centre, Budbrooke Road, Warwick CV34 5WE, England
Tel. 01926 499 619
Email: info@helion.co.uk Website: www.helion.co.uk Twitter: @helionbooks Visit our blog http://blog.helion.co.uk/

Published by Helion & Company 2021
Designed and typeset by Farr out Publications, Wokingham, Berkshire
Cover designed by Paul Hewitt, Battlefield Design (www.battlefield-design.co.uk)

ISBN 978-1-914377-16-7

British Library Cataloguing-in-Publication Data.
A catalogue record for this book is available from the British Library.

For details of other military history titles published by Helion & Company Limited contact the above address, or visit our website: http://www.helion.co.uk. We always welcome receiving book proposals from prospective authors.

ABBREVIATIONS

A.A.	anti-aircraft
ACAS	Assistant Chief of the Air Staff
AOC	Air Officer Commanding
ATFC	Air Task Force Commander
AUW	all up weight (take-off weight of an aircraft)
BDA	bomb damage assessment
BS	Blue Shadow (sidescan radar on Canberra bomber)
BTR	basic training requirement
C-in-C	Commander-in-Chief
CAS	Chief of the Air Staff (chief of air force)
COS	Chief-of-Staff (the head of all branches of armed forces)
CRT	cathode ray tube (electronic display; for example for a radar system)
DZ	drop zone (for paratroopers)
EAF	Egyptian Air Force
F1/F2	first and second crews dropping flares (there could be up to four)
GA	ground attack
GEE	navigation system
GEE-H (or G-H)	bombing system using GEE
GMT/ZULU	Greenwich Mean Time (time-zone)
H2S	radar component of the Navigation Bombing System
HE	high explosive
HF	high frequency (radio communication system)
HQ	headquarters
IP	initial point (last navigation waypoint before target)
JARIC	Joint Air Reconnaissance Centre
LABS	low altitude bombing system (enabling so-called 'toss bombing')
M1/M2	Marker 1/Marker 2 (there could be up to four)
MEAF	Middle East Air Force
NBS	navigation bombing system (in Valiant bomber)
OC	Officer Commanding
OCU	Operational Conversion Unit
ORB	Operations Record Book
PM	Prime Minister
PR	photo reconnaissance
RT	radio transmission
Sqn Ldr	Squadron Leader
T4/T14	variants of visual bombing sights
TI	target indicator
TNA	The National Archives (in Kew, UK)
TOT or H-Hour	Time on Target
U.E.	unit establishment
UN	United Nations
VCAS	Vice-Chief of the Air Staff
VHF/HF	very high frequency (radio communication systems)
VT	variable time fuse (on a bomb)
Wg Cdr	Wing Commander

ACKNOWLEDGEMENTS.

This book could not have been written without access to the documents held at the National Archive in Kew. I am especially grateful to the TNA for allowing the free download of digitised files during the period of the pandemic. Without this facility, it would not have been possible to complete the work during the various Covid-19 'lockdowns'. I am also enormously grateful to those who helped me to 'flesh out' the official reports with access to notes or logbooks from some of those who flew bombing missions over Egypt. Henry Horscroft and Howard Jones allowed me to use the account written by Fred Jones (Howard's father), printed in the 44 (Rhodesia) Squadron newsletter. Howard also sent me a photo of Fred and another of his logbook for the appropriate dates. I would also like to thank Henry for putting my request for information in the squadron newsletter. The Royal Air Force Historical Society also has my thanks for allowing me to use some of the articles in their journal. Information and photos on the websites of Rob Mather and Don Chadwick (both listed in the bibliography) are also gratefully acknowledged. George Perrin was good enough to answer some of my questions by telephone and John King was good enough to enlighten me on some of the mysteries of Blue Shadow, as well as sending me a copy of a technical paper on this equipment. Tom Cooper has done a great job with the artwork on the cover and throughout the book. An old school friend, Peter Smith, was 10 when his family was part of the 1956 withdrawal from Egypt to Cyprus (prior to Musketeer) and his emails have been an encouragement during this year of Covid-19. I am especially grateful to Roger Green – a retired Wing Commander and ex Canberra navigator – for his technical support during the project, for casting a technical eye over the draft of the manuscript, and for the company of himself and Jane at a number of lunches with my wife and myself at the Royal Air Force Club. Any remaining errors in this account are of course my own.

I should state at this point that I was a Navigator/Radar on Vulcan bombers in the early 1970s, on 27, 44 and 101 Squadrons. These were the years prior to digital computers and GPS, a time when the Vulcan's Navigation and Bombing System (NBS) was considered 'up to date'.

1

INTRODUCTION

On the evening of 26 July 1956, the British Prime Minister, Sir Anthony Eden, was hosting a dinner at 10 Downing Street for King Faisal of Iraq and his Prime Minister Nuri es-Said. At about 10.15 p.m., Eden was handed a message by the duty secretary: Gamal Abdel Nasser, the President of Egypt, had nationalised the Suez Canal Company. From this point on Eden determined that Britain, as yet unwilling to come to terms with its post-war loss of empire, would not take this assault on British strategic interests lying down. Unfortunately, his decision led to his name being forever associated with a campaign that had more of the smell of nineteenth century colonialism than 20th century diplomacy.

The Canal was opened on 17 November 1869 and provided a vital (and much shorter) route to Britain's interests in India and the Far East. In 1875, Benjamin Disraeli's government took a 44 percent share in the Suez Canal Company, a private enterprise that operated (but did not own) the Canal. The point is important,

At least from the official British point of view, the nation's primary interest in involvement in Egypt – and thus the primary reason for involvement in the tripartite aggression of 1956 – was the Suez Canal. This photograph shows a view from north to south. Barely visible in the centre left is the Firdan Railway Bridge (in open condition), completed in 1918. (Albert Grandolini Collection)

as Britain had never bought a 44 percent stake in the Canal, only in the operating company. However, that did not stop British troops being sent to Alexandria and Port Said in 1882 to defend what London saw as its 'interest in the Canal Zone'. From this point on Britain operated a 'veiled protectorate' in Egypt.[1] The strategic importance of the Canal increased with the discovery of oil in the Middle East, and its rapid adoption by the Royal Navy as fuel for its warships in place of coal.

Through the early decades of the 20th century, up to the crisis in 1956, Britain had a history of meddling in the Middle East: the Sykes-Picot agreement; Palestine and the creation of Israel; Lawrence of Arabia; the Balfour Declaration, carving out new states and defence agreements with the various Arab nations in the region. In 1936, Eden was the Foreign Secretary who helped to negotiate an Anglo-Egyptian Treaty of Friendship and Alliance, which allowed for the stationing of 10,000 British troops in the Canal Zone.[2] Not surprisingly by the beginning of the 1950s, the British presence was seen as a form of occupation and a target for nationalists and the Muslim Brotherhood alike. As unrest grew and outbreaks of violence against the troops increased, Britain raised the number of soldiers in the Canal Zone to 80,000 – eight times more than Eden's agreement of 1936 allowed for.[3]

The years after the Second World War were difficult for a Britain trying to come to terms with its loss of empire and the movements for decolonisation; it was no longer acceptable to continue to act in Egypt as an Imperial occupier. On 19 October 1954, the British government signed an agreement that all troops would be withdrawn from the Canal Zone by 18 June 1956. By 12.15 on 13 June, just six weeks before Eden received the note in 10 Downing Street, the last troops had left Port Said. Now, if the government decided to take military action against Egypt, the only forces available in the Mediterranean were those stationed in Cyprus, and they were only equipped to counter the long-running problems between the Turks and Greeks on that island, not an amphibious operation at Alexandria or Port Said.

The early 1950s were the start of the Cold War between the two competing superpowers, America and Russia. Meanwhile Britain, also a nuclear power following its test of an atomic bomb on 3 October 1952, was struggling to reconcile itself to its reduced economic and political power in the world. Egypt was able to take advantage of the struggle between the competing ideologies of Washington and Moscow by pitting one against the other in Cairo's wish to buy arms and finance the Aswan Dam project. Nasser gave the West the opportunity to help him with both the arms and the dam. A request for $100 million in arms met with a response of only $20 million while both America and Britain withdrew from previous 'agreements' to help to fund the dam. In the event, Russian arms (including Il-28 jet bombers and MiG fighters, which would present threats during the 1956 crisis) were supplied via Czechoslovakia. Nasser took the West's withdrawal of funding for his dam as a comment on Egyptian economic competence and decided that he would fund it from the proceeds of nationalising the Suez Canal Company. It is important for what happened later to note that Nasser was not intending to stop international shipping from using the Canal; he only wanted to take it under Egyptian control. In the heated rhetoric of the day, the average newspaper reader on the Clapham omnibus might have been forgiven for thinking that Nasser was stopping British ships from using this strategic waterway.

Only 10 years after being on the 'winning' side in the Second World War, with a seat on the United Nations Security Council and having exploded its own nuclear weapon, was Britain going to be dictated to by Egypt? Eden was a seasoned politician who had spent years in the shadow of Churchill and by the time that he became Prime Minister, he was not a well man. Whether because of his illness, or because he felt let down by Nasser after the 1954 agreement, he made a number of errors in his handling of the situation; he completely misread the attitude of Eisenhower's administration (it was election year in the USA), and he allowed Britain's response to have something of the ring of an old colonial power. Sir Humphrey Trevelyan, Britain's Ambassador to Cairo, summed it up well:

As of 1956, the Suez Canal was still relatively narrow, which meant that ships had to move in convoy in one direction, while those travelling the other way had to wait their turn. This photograph shows a line of merchant ships along the bank of the Great Bitter Lake, waiting for their opportunity to exit in the southern direction. (Albert Grandolini Collection)

> There was truth in the old saying that in the Middle East the British never saw the writing on the wall until they hit their heads against it; […] our difficulties were due to our inability to realise that we were not living in the nineteenth century and no longer had the power to enable us to keep the Middle East as our political preserve.[4]

The assessment of the historian Corelli Barnett was a little pithier; Eden's actions were 'the dithers of a bishop nerving himself to enter a brothel'.[5]

It should be made clear at this point that this account is not a comprehensive detailing of the politics behind Britain's intervention in Suez, nor does it attempt to detail all the military action that involved the RAF, the Navy and the Army. This book is limited to the bombing campaign of the bomber wings on Malta and Cyprus and the political manoeuvrings as they affected the planning of this campaign.

2

EDEN WANTS ACTION

Following the dinner on 26 July and the news of Nasser's nationalisation of the Canal, Eden called a meeting with his Chiefs of Staff. While the PM wanted rapid military action, the Chiefs told him that time was needed to prepare the operation that would be required. As we have already noted, the force in the Mediterranean was intended to counter the troubles among the Cypriot community, not to launch an amphibious operation against Egypt. However, although diplomatic efforts to resolve the issue would be attempted (if a little disingenuously) the Chiefs of Staff (COS) were told to prepare a plan for the 'retaking' of the Canal. Eden told the Cabinet on 27 July that the military planning should be 'on [the] worst [case] basis – viz., action alone'.[1] At this early stage in the planning, Eden demonstrated his misjudgement of the Americans: he told the Cabinet that 'as on prev. [sic] occasions U.S. wd. [sic] follow our lead if we took it'. Demonstrating his animosity towards the Egyptian leader, Eden spelled out the object of the proposed military action; 'elimination of N[asser]'. Already, on 30 July 1956, the Egypt Committee – set up to handle the growing crisis – was suggesting that at some point Nasser would be sent a 'virtual ultimatum' and if he refused to accept it, 'military operations would then proceed'.[2] As mentioned above, the Cabinet decided on 27 July that military force would be used; 'Whatever it may cost, we have no alternative' and although the Eisenhower administration would claim to have been unaware of Britain's intentions, that is not correct. After the meeting, Eden wrote to the American President; 'My colleagues and I are convinced that we must be ready, in the last resort, to use force to bring Nasser to his senses. For our part we are prepared to do so'.[3]

Although the Cabinet had indicated their willingness to use force there is one comment in the minutes that appears to have escaped the notice of other historians' accounts. Sir Dermot Boyle, Chief of the Air Staff (CAS) asked 'Are we to use a. bombs. W[d]. [sic, *would*] simplify it for us. They are available'.[4] Boyle's reference is to atomic bombs and this may have been missed because they are normally referred to as 'A bombs' rather than 'a. bombs'. This is not the only reference to this class of weapon. In the National Archive at Kew, one of the files holding papers relating to Operation Musketeer (the operations against Egypt) outlined the RAF resources that could be available, including 'special weapons' – the RAF term for nuclear bombs. Thirty-one were available, each with a yield of 10 Kilotons and '31 aircraft could drop weapon (some air and some ground burst)'.[5] These aircraft were the Valiant V-bombers. It is incredible that the use of these weapons was even part of the conversation on operations against Egypt.

THE WHIFF OF COLLUSION

When Eden's government decided to take action against Nasser, they were well aware that their grounds for doing so were thin, Nasser was not closing the Canal, he was simply nationalising the Canal Company, which was a legally registered Egyptian company. Britain needed a pretext for military action and while Eden was prepared to go it alone, he preferred to act alongside France.

While the British government's aggressive stance towards Nasser was primarily based on their perception of the threat to the Canal, and so to British oil supplies and the route to India, the French government of Guy Mollet had a different concern namely, Egyptian support of the Algerian National Liberation Front. In the months following the Downing Street meeting in July until British bombs began to fall on Egypt on 31 October, planning would take place on the political and the military levels.

This account does not attempt to detail all the political and diplomatic steps that preceded the outbreak of hostilities; these are admirably covered in accounts listed in the bibliography, with those by Kyle and Tunzelmann especially recommended by this author. However, the underhand way in which Britain became involved with Israel in the attack on Egypt is pertinent to the opening phases of the military operation.

One of the complications for Britain, both politically and militarily, was the defence treaty with Jordan (1948), which guaranteed support for that country against any aggressor and so could be invoked if Israel took military action in the West Bank. The existence of this treaty together with the complications that would arise with any Israeli involvement in military action by Britain and France, were of importance during the military planning and the opening phase of the operation. The treaty came close to being invoked in mid-October as a result of an Israeli reprisal raid into Jordan following the murder of some Israeli workers.

France could not afford to have Britain being drawn into a conflict with Israel if the Israelis were the intended ally of France during any action against Nasser; Mollet had to bring Eden in on the French plan. On 14 October, Major General Maurice Challe and the French Minister of Social Affairs, Albert Gazier, met Eden and members of his Cabinet at Chequers. This was the start of the discussions that would result in the Sèvres Protocol. Over the next 10 days, Britain agreed to join in a duplicitous arrangement with France and Israel for an attack on Egypt: Israel would attack through the Sinai then Britain and France, feigning no prior knowledge of the incursion, would intercede with an ultimatum requiring both Israel and Egypt to withdraw their forces. When Israel did invade, Eden sent a lying telegram to Eisenhower in which he claimed that Britain 'would not wish to support or even condone the action of Israel'.[6]

Should the ultimatum be rejected by the Egyptians – and it would be framed to ensure that they did – then Britain and France would go in to secure the Canal Zone. The Israeli Prime Minister, David Ben Gurion, wanted the British, French and Israeli attacks to start at the same time but Eden favoured the Anglo-French entry being two days later so that the Israeli invasion would serve as his 'pretext'. Ben Gurion was very concerned that this delay would expose Israeli cities to Egyptian bombing.

On 24 October, Patrick Dean (a minister at the Foreign Office) was sent to Sèvres for the final meeting where he signed the Protocol on behalf of Eden's government. Dean signed the agreement *ad referendum*, meaning that Eden would have to signify agreement to it. The Prime Minister did so in a veiled comment to Mollet, which did not specify the details of the agreement, the British Government 'confirm that in the situation there envisaged [at Sèvres on 24 October] they will take the action described'.[7] When Eden learned on Dean's return of the written copies of the agreement, he sent Dean back to try to recover the British copy and to have France and Israel destroy theirs. He was too late; history had a record of this less than noble arrangement. Britain does not come well out of the Suez operation and as we will see, the politicians' wish for secrecy over the collusion with Israel had repercussions on the military planning and the bombing

This photo shows a meeting between Anthony Eden and Gamal Abdel Nasser, the Egyptian President, in Cairo in 1955. Eden spoke classical Arabic but Nasser was less impressed with the fact that the British attended in dinner jackets, this offended his Arab nationalist views and caused him to state afterwards that it smacked of colonialism. (Albert Grandolini Collection)

campaign. On the same day that the Sèvres Protocol was finalised, Soviet troops moved into Budapest; this was after all the Cold War.

Eden must have been living in a world of his own if he believed that his government's duplicity would not one day see the light of day. On 25 October, Anthony Nutting (a minister at the Foreign Office who later resigned over Eden's policy) was told by Lloyd that he – Lloyd – 'must call a meeting to draft the ultimatum which we shall be sending out';[8] this was the British response to the Israeli 'surprise' action that would take place four days later.

3

BRITISH MILITARY PLANNING

Britain's involvement in the Middle East had become more strategic with the discovery of oil in the region, and the Royal Navy's need for the new fuel. Given the importance of the Arab countries to Britain's geo-strategic priorities, it will be no surprise to the reader that the military had various plans in place for different possible scenarios based on Britain's treaties with those Arab states. Reference has already been made to the Anglo-Jordanian treaty and the possible need to defend that country against Israel. None of those plans was based on the need to invade Egypt.

The nearest RAF base to any possible area of conflict in the Eastern Mediterranean in the early 1950s was Nicosia on the island of Cyprus, where the attention of the British was focused on the internecine warfare between the Turkish and Greek Cypriots; EOKA terrorism, Enosis (the movement for union with Greece) and the eventual need for Eden to deport Archbishop Makarios to the Seychelles in March 1956. Following the agreement to withdraw British troops from the Canal Zone, RAF planners drew up two plans based on the assumption that Israel would be the enemy in any Middle East conflict, TASMAN and ALACRITY.[1] The first involved Canberra bombers operating from Nicosia and Kasfareet (an airfield in Egypt) against the Israelis – there was no thought of Egypt as the target. The second detailed the planning for the dispersal, maintenance and operation of an augmented Canberra force to operate under Tasman. Alacrity would be central to the movement of RAF forces deployed to the Mediterranean for the operations against Egypt in October 1956.

The planning for the operation began immediately after Nasser's nationalisation of the Canal but the work was hampered by Eden's need to keep secret the collusion between the participants; all operational orders 'were conditioned by the political need for them to be consistent with the cover story'[2] and, although the date of the Israeli attack was known beforehand, it was necessary for the Anglo-French reaction to appear to be that of impartial peace-keepers towards a 'surprise' attack. As Keith Kyle put it, 'it was impossible to have the armada just over the horizon'. According to Sir Frank Cooper (head of the Air Staff Secretariat in 1956), there was great confusion in the Air Ministry, 'nobody really knew what the aim was. Were we supposed to go and capture the whole of Egypt? Were we supposed to hold the Canal Zone?' In Cooper's opinion, the Secretary of State for Air 'knew absolutely nothing about the whole subject. [...] He was never really in the picture other than being confused'.[3] Sir Denis Smallwood was Group Captain (Plans) in the Air Task Force and made the damning comment that the basis on which the planners had to work was one of 'monumental cock-up',[4] while Sir David Lee, Secretary to the Chiefs of Staff Committee at the time, stated that he was forbidden from attending the meeting of the Chiefs at Downing Street; something which he says was 'unprecedented'.[5] There are times when the need to know can be taken too far.

While confusion was the order of the day at Ministry level, further down the chain Canberra bombers were assigned to the operation, to be operated from Luqa in Malta as well as Nicosia

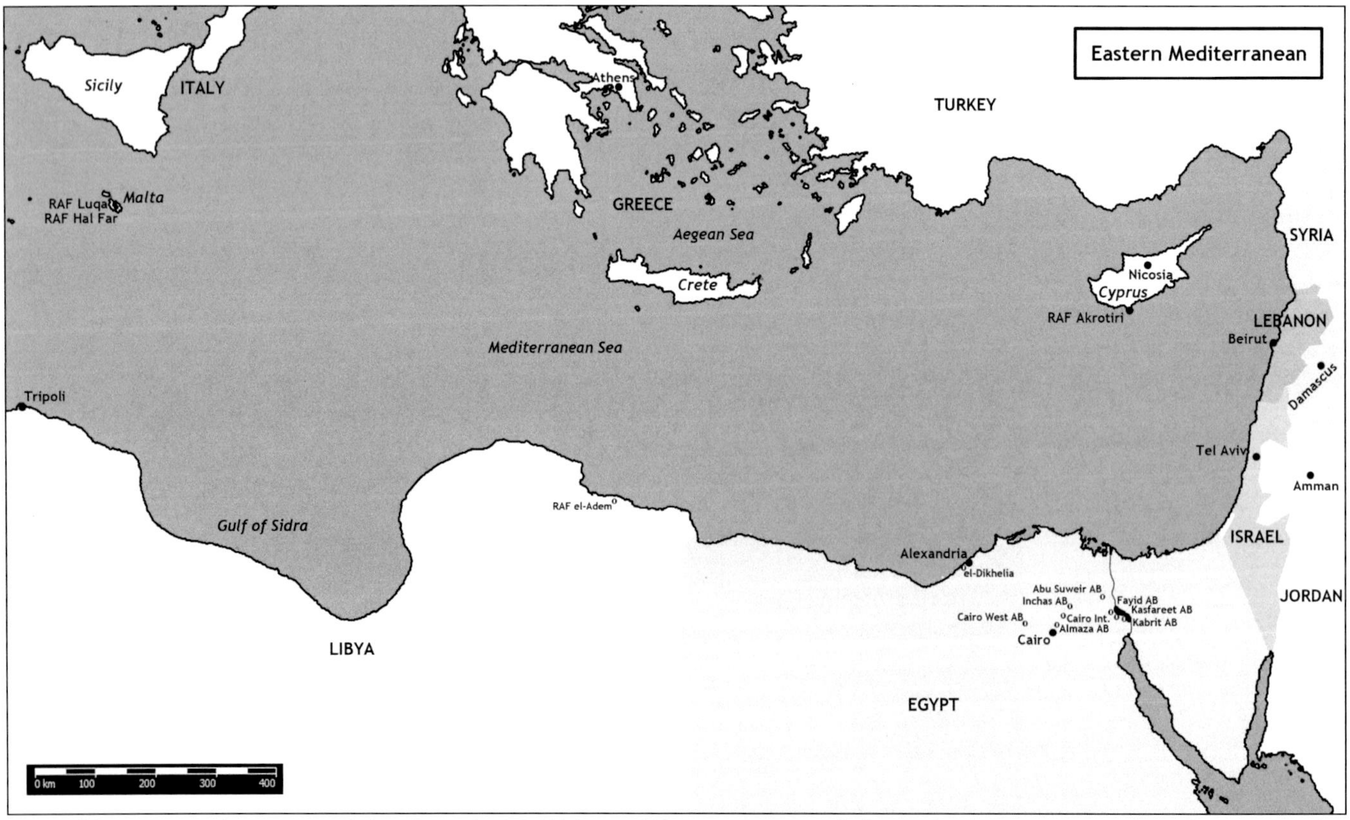

A map of the Eastern Mediterranean, including Cyprus (with British bases of Akrotiri and Nicosia, which were the closest to Egypt), Malta and Lower Egypt, the main focus of Operation Musketeer. (Map by Tom Cooper)

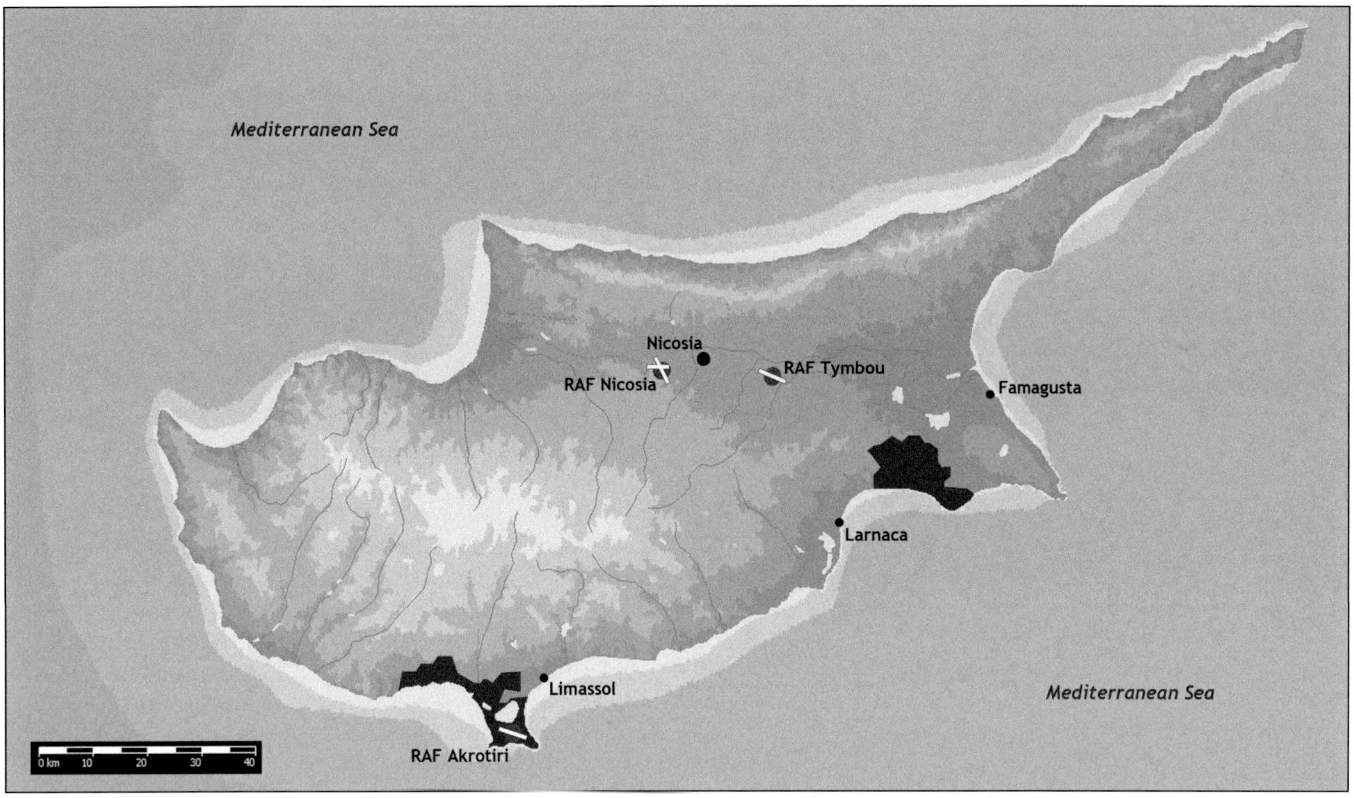

British bases on Cyprus as of 1956 included RAF Akrotiri (still in use until today), RAF Nicosia and RAF Tymbou. (Map by Tom Cooper)

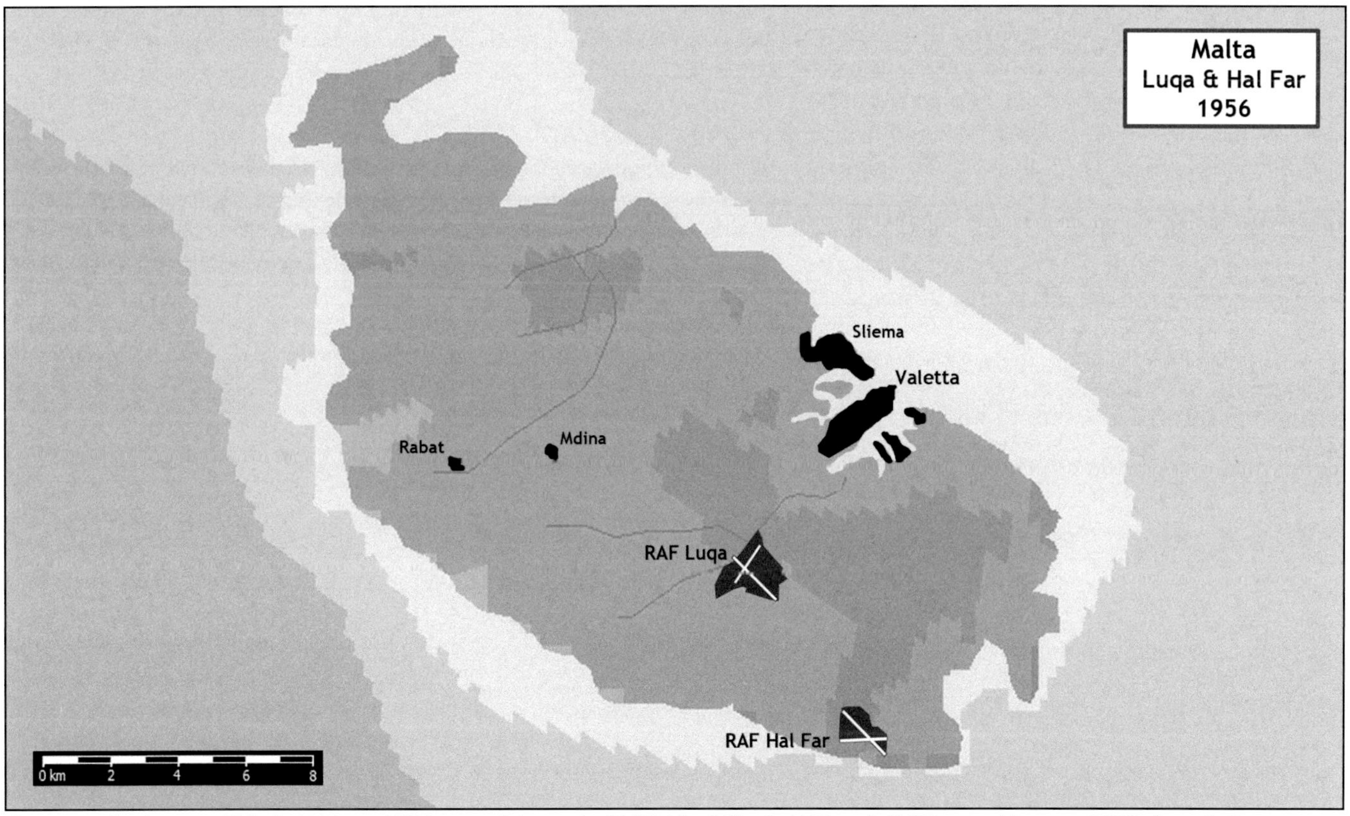

The principal air bases on Malta in 1956 were RAF Luqa and the nearby RAF Hal Far. Still only 1,776 yards (1,639 metres) long as of 1952, the main Runway 24/06 at Luqa was the reason for several fatal accidents. Consequently, it was resurfaced during the same year and then extended to 1,960 yards (1,792 metres) by 1956, enabling operations of Valiant and Canberra bombers. Runway 14/32 and the nearby RAF Hal Far were used by the resident squadrons and civilian operators during the reconstructions of the main runway at Luqa in the 1952-1956 period, and then again once the decision was taken in 1957 to extend its main runway to 2,660 yards (2,377 metres). (Map by Tom Cooper)

in Cyprus. Additionally Valiant (V-bombers) would be based at Luqa. Early plans envisioned their being based at Idris, Hal Far and Aden but these were ruled out for political reasons. Similarly, the Foreign Office ruled out the use of El Adem in Libya.

With the decision having been made to take action against Nasser's nationalisation of the Canal, the military planners had to get on with it. Unaware of the collusion agreed at Sèvres, the proposal (Operation Musketeer) was for initial air attacks to neutralise the Egyptian Air Force (EAF), thus allowing an

The crew of a 40mm Bofors anti-aircraft gun seen in its position on Cyprus in 1956. (Albert Grandolini Collection)

amphibious assault on Alexandria and a subsequent drive for the Canal Zone. This 'was discarded in late August for political reasons'[6] – the fear of severe civilian casualties – and partly because it would involve overt troop movements 'at politically awkward times'. The second iteration of the plan was Musketeer Revise, and this was the operational plan in force when the military action began. However, as Air Marshall Barnett's report went on to state, it was 'dictated to the Force Commanders as the result of political limitations and was never considered by them to be a sound military operation'; the auguries for Musketeer Revise were not good.

The revised plan retained the RAF objective of neutralising the EAF (Phase I), followed by air attacks against other selected targets and 'a psychological warfare campaign designed to reduce the Egyptian will to resist' (Phase II).[7] The landing at Alexandria (which was considered to cause too many civilian deaths) was replaced by an airborne assault on Port Said (Phase III) with a build-up and break-out down the length of the Canal. Barnett's report makes the point that the minimising of the loss of civilian lives imposed restrictions on the use of the air forces, 'even at the expense of operational effectiveness'.

The critical importance of the role of the Air Force to the operation was spelled out in the report by the Joint Planning Staff, 1 August 1956:

> In this connection [air operations] it cannot be too highly stressed that the air action is the cornerstone of the entire concept as the forces which can be used in an assault are too small to deal with any determined opposition. If troops are to be landed air action, bombing and ground attack must already have been sufficiently effective to allow them more or less to walk ashore. If for any reason a sufficiently massive air attack cannot be launched, the entire operation is liable to fail.[8]

Most official documents and histories of the conflict drop *Revise* from the name of the operation and simply call it *Musketeer*; this account will adopt that convention for subsequent pages.

COMMAND STRUCTURE

The three Chiefs of Staff during Musketeer were, Admiral Earl Mountbatten, General Sir Gerald Templer and Air Chief Marshal Sir Dermot Boyle. Overall command on the ground was vested in General Sir Giles Keightley as Commander-in-Chief (C-in-C)

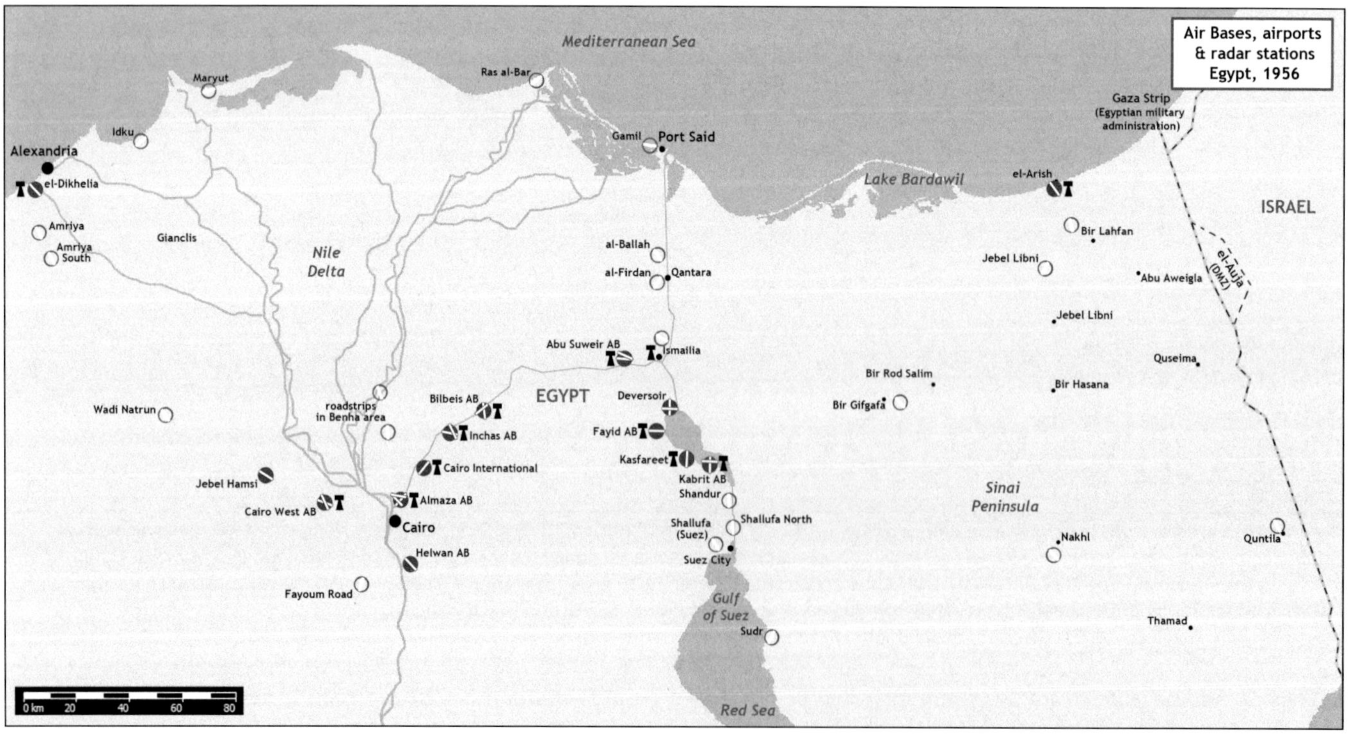

This map shows the air bases, airports and radar stations in Lower Egypt as of late October 1956. Unknown to the British and their allies – whose reconnaissance flights had found next to no activity only a month earlier – by the time of Musketeer a team of Czechoslovak advisors had significantly improved the early warning radar system of the EAF: this was tied into a fighter control system, capable of guiding MiG interceptors against high-flying bombers by night. Once Operation Musketeer was initiated, this operational improvement came as a rude surprise to the RAF. (Map by Tom Cooper)

Middle East Land Forces; the Air Task Force Commander was Air Marshal Barnett. Although the Middle East Air Force (MEAF) had a commander and a staff in Cyprus (Air Marshall Sir Hubert Patch), he had his hands full with the defence of Cyprus during the on-going EOKA troubles. While the army took out key members of an existing staff to run their side of Musketeer, Barnett's staff was formed from scratch. The formation of a new staff group caused some issues as it conflicted with that already existing in Air HQ Levant 'with responsibilities very similar to those of the new Air Task Force'.[9] The RAF approach to the formation of the staff group did have the disadvantage of rubbing up against AHQ Levant, and was slower coming together than the Navy and Army staffs, but it did have the advantage that it allowed for the individual selection of first class officers.

An aerial view of RAF Luqa as of the early 1960s, from the southern direction. At the time, the base was not much different to its condition in 1956 though it probably did not have Park 4, visible on the right side, left of Runway 06/24. (Richard Caruana Collection)

We have already seen from earlier comments that the planning between July and October was chaotic, with most of those concerned only being privy to some of the details, especially regarding Israel. The Israelis invaded Egypt on the night of 28/29 October with the result that the Staff Groups who had expected to be in Cyprus on D-Day minus 10 (D-10) suddenly found the timescales truncated so that they were actually at D-3, 'without any official knowledge that his [Barnett's] units were at anything other than the normal ten days' notice which had been in force for the past six weeks'.[10] One serious operational consequence (outlined in the Air Task Force Commander's report) was that essential photographic reconnaissance, which should have started on D-8, had not taken place and 'there was little time to develop the correct techniques for selecting, processing and interpreting top priority negatives'. It was becoming obvious that all involved would have to demonstrate initiative and creative thinking if the operation was to be successful.

4

RESOURCES AVAILABLE

Because this account of the Suez operation is limited to the RAF bombing campaign, there will be no mention of the contribution made by the French air force, the Fleet Air Arm or the fighters and ground attack aircraft of the RAF based on Cyprus.[1] This account will be limited to those sorties flown by the Canberras and Valiants in theatre in support of Musketeer.

An aerial view of RAF Hal Far as of the early 1960s, as seen from the north-western direction. (Richard Caruana Collection)

had Nicosia (the main one) and Akrotiri. Nicosia required essential repair work doing to one of its runways, but it was anticipated that this would be completed in time to allow two-runway operation from 15 August. To overcome the concerns regarding the air defence, two squadrons of Hawker Hunter F5 fighters were sent to Nicosia under Operation Quickfire.[3]

An important question for the planners was where the bombers should be based. Ideally, they needed to be within operational range of their targets, but either outside the range of Egyptian bombers and ground attack aircraft, or on a base with adequate anti-aircraft defences. Cyprus met the range requirement but did not have the capacity to accept them all, and there were questions over its defence. Malta met the defence requirement, being outside the range of EAF aircraft, but was on the limits of the operational range of the Canberras. The solution was to split the bomber force into Cyprus and Malta wings. Although the Canberras at Luqa would need to monitor their fuel states closely, because of the range, it was the better base for the Valiants. As these were Britain's new V-bombers, the Air Staff would be reluctant to base them within range of EAF aircraft, and they would also be operating at night to lessen the risk of losses. However, alternative bases were considered. The HQ at MEAF

By 30 July, only four days after Eden received the news of Nasser's action, the Air Ministry was sending out signals for the deployment of the Canberras and Valiants to Malta and Cyprus. However, at the same time MEAF was reminding the Air Ministry of its concerns that Cyprus had 'limited capacity' to operate large air forces because of its 'sketchy air defence arrangements' and minimum facilities for the control and recovery of large numbers of aircraft in short time-frames.[2] In spite of this, Malta and Cyprus would be the two main RAF bases. Both of these islands had two airfields; Malta had Luqa (the main one) and Hal Far; Cyprus

A line-up of Gloster Meteor FR.Mk 9 reconnaissance fighters from No. 208 Squadron, seen at RAF Hal Far during the Suez Campaign. While providing air defence over Malta they still received 'Suez Stripes' for easier identification. (Malta Aviation Museum Foundation via Richard Caruana)

With Cyprus being within the range of Egyptian Il-28s, air defence of the local air bases were reinforced with two squadrons of Hunter F.Mk 1 interceptors. (Albert Grandolini Collection)

signalled the Air Ministry on 30 July that they could accommodate a flight of four Valiants at Bahrein and four at Aden but suggested that operating bombers from Bahrein against Egypt might result in 'political objections, leading to unrest' and it might be better to base all eight aircraft at Aden.[4] In the event, neither base was used. The RAF had a large base at El Adem in Libya (this author had the dubious pleasure of spending New Year there in 1963), but it was within range of the Russian Il-28 (NATO name Beagle) bombers operated by the Egyptians. From an operational viewpoint, El Adem had the advantage that, while within Il-28 range, it was a little less than half the distance that the Luqa aircraft would have to fly to Egyptian targets. The legal advice to the Foreign Office was that any build-up of forces on Libyan soil without Libyan permission, or operations from Libyan bases, 'would be entirely against International law'; in their view, operating from Libya 'would be tantamount to taking the country over'.[5] Like Bahrein and Aden, El Adem was not used during the Suez operation.

Modern conflicts in the Gulf have demonstrated that the Services usually have to call on reservists to fill essential non-combatant support roles. That was also the case in 1956. At a

This photograph nicely illustrates both the clean lines of the Canberra bomber and its low ground clearance. Also notable is the transparent nose cone for the bomb aimer, and for visual navigation. (Albert Grandolini Collection)

A Canberra B(I).Mk 8 bomber from No. 16 Squadron (then home-based at Laarbruch, in West Germany) seen during a temporary detachment in the Middle East, together with local camel-mounted troops. (Albert Grandolini Collection)

A Vickers Valiant B.Mk 1 bomber seen at a base in the UK. Visible in front and under the wing is the ground handling equipment. (John Dillon Collection)

A trio of Valiants passing low over Buckingham Palace during a military parade in June 1956. (Albert Grandolini Collection)

Cabinet meeting on 2 August,[6] it was decided that a proclamation should be issued for the call up of 8,000 Class B Reserves to fill specialist roles in ports and docks. As well as personnel, additional ships would need to be requisitioned for the transport of lorries, troops and ground equipment (as happened during the Falklands War). However, reservists cannot be taken away from their regular jobs for long periods and the condition of vehicles kept on ships without being used, deteriorates. With the crisis approaching, but the troops not yet having been used, Eden told the Cabinet on 23 October[7] that the military forces could not be held much longer 'at their present state of readiness'; to use a modern idiom, they had to 'use them, or lose them'. At this point, the war was only a week away, but the commanders on the ground were still unaware of the whole picture.

Operation Musketeer was an opportunity for the RAF to 'blood' their newest jet bombers, the Canberra (B.1 and B.6 variants) and the first of the three V-bombers, the Valiant. The Canberra was born out of a requirement to replace the Second World War Mosquito with a high-level, jet powered aircraft, capable of visual bombing and with its high performance as its only defence. The Valiant had been designed to meet a quite different requirement; it was to carry the British nuclear deterrent as a strategic, long-range bomber against the Soviet Union. The advantage it had over the Canberra at Suez was its greater operational range and much larger bomb load.

CANBERRA

The B1 and B2 variants both had a three-man crew of pilot, navigator and observer/bomb aimer. This made for a tight fit, with the navigator and observer seats being in a 'cubby hole' behind the pilot, with very limited light or visibility. Bomb aiming was done from a prone position in the nose, with its transparent nose cone. This author had an exciting familiarisation sortie at low level in a B.6 in Germany in 1968, spending the whole trip in the prone position. Both variants were powered by two Rolls Royce Avons, the B.2 having the 101 version with 6,500lb static thrust while the B.6 had the more powerful Avon 109 with 7,500lb static thrust. Both models had internal bomb bays capable of carrying 6,000 pounds, which could be a mix of bombs, flares and Target Indicators, depending on the sortie to be flown. The combat radius of the Canberra B.2 (with a 6,000lb load) was only 820 nautical miles (nm),[8] which could be extended by the addition of 2 x 244 gallon jettisonable wing-tip tanks.[9] This range limitation did present problems as the straight-line distance between Luqa and Cairo was 1,115 nm.[10]

VALIANT

The Vickers Valiant was a much larger aircraft than the Canberra, with a crew of five (pilot, co-pilot, navigator, navigator/bomb aimer and air electronics officer), four engines and a possible bomb load of 21 x 1,000lb bombs, although they only carried 12 x 1,000lb on their Suez sorties. With a load of 10,000lb, they had a combat radius of 1,155 nm.[11] The Valiant was designed to drop a nuclear bomb, using the Navigation Bombing System (NBS). This delivery system used a development of the Second World War H2S radar for bomb aiming, feeding inputs to an analogue computing system which took account of aircraft height, speed and bomb ballistics to produce a forward throw for the weapon, and the consequent bomb release point. Unfortunately, as we will see, NBS had reliability problems and not all Valiants deployed for Suez had the NBS fit.

Lines of conventional (or 'dumb') bombs. The examples already on the trolley have their tail units attached: those lined up on the ground are waiting for theirs to be fitted. (Albert Grandolini Collection)

BOMB STOCKS

It would be a truism to say that, to have a bombing operation, you need bombs. Since the first Gulf War in 1991/92 we have become used to the idea of modern air forces dropping precision, laser-guided bombs. While some might impact wide of the target, the majority are incredibly accurate; this was not the case in October 1956. The bombs carried by the Canberras and Valiants at Suez were 'dumb', free-fall munitions of the type used in the Second World War and while large stocks were available, they came in a number of varieties. In simple terms, a bomb has three parts: the nose section, which frequently (but not always) contains the fusing unit; the mid-section, which is a heavy steel container for the explosive material; and the tail unit, which is relatively light in weight and designed to give the bomb its ballistic profile. The three sections each had different variants so that certain bomb units could not be matched with different tail units, and only certain combinations could be loaded onto our two aircraft types. This meant that large numbers of bombs and tail units had to be located and ferried to Luqa and Nicosia for the intended bombing operation. By the time that Musketeer was launched the required bomb combinations were in place, but it is worth mentioning some of the issues facing the armourers during the deployment phase:

> While Nicosia held 3,500 x 1,000lb bombs (not enough to begin a war) the UK had a stock of 27,000 'but only 280 tails designed for high speed, high altitude dropping'. However, there were a further 18,000 No.100 Mark 6 tails 'which it is considered could be used provided they were fitted with a lanyard to open the tail'.
>
> While these 18,000 tail units would enable the Mark 6/9 bomb to be carried by the Canberra, a No.107 Mark 2 tail unit (of which Boscombe Down and Marham held only 284) was needed for the same bomb to be loaded on a Valiant.[12]

The bombs to be used for Musketeer were the Mark 6 with the type 100 tail unit, a 'high speed, high altitude weapon, which when fitted with the No. 100 tail imposes no height or speed limitations on the dropping aircraft'.[13] Between the UK depots and Nicosia, 21,500 of these bomb/tail units were available, but large numbers would need to be moved quickly to theatre.

The bomb stocks required in the Middle East were based on the original plans for Alacrity and on this basis the 3,500 at Nicosia were to be augmented by 3,204 at Malta and 2,184 at Idris (Libya) or 'alternative airfield'; in the event, Idris was not used. These stocks would prove more than adequate, but a ferry programme would need to be implemented to reach these levels. Two ships were earmarked, the SS *Jessmon* and the SS *Anatolian*, for loading during August at London and Milford Haven respectively. Meanwhile, 1,008 of the bombs would be ferried out to Luqa by Canberras; the intention was to achieve this in one week, at the rate of 144 bombs per day. With each aircraft able to carry six bombs, that would entail 24 aircraft every day for seven days, the aircraft arriving in pairs at two-hour intervals.[14] Flying Officer F.H. Jones was a Canberra pilot on 44 Squadron and he wrote that 'between 2-11 August, 44 Squadron alone made a total of 29 trips with each aircraft carrying 6 x 1,000lb bombs. For two weeks during August all the Honington squadrons were involved in daily return flights to Malta'.[15]

The detailed planning for the necessary bomb stocks was best left to the Logistics Officers, who might have had a wry smile at one very senior officer's involvement. On 31 July, the Assistant Chief of the Air Staff (ACAS) submitted a memo that added nothing to the planning process. He wanted to make people aware of the 'situation regarding 12,000lb, and 22,000lb H.E. bombs';[16] these were the Tallboy and Grand Slam bombs used by Lancasters towards the end of the Second World War. The ACAS had not put a lot of thought into the subject before sending his memo: of the 360 Tallboys available, only 25 had serviceable tail units, while only 52 tails could be found for the 126 Grand Slams, and of these 52, only one was serviceable. As the Canberra could only carry a load of 6,000lb, both weapons were outside its capacity and the ACAS went on to state that, 'I understand that the above mentioned bombs and tail units could not be released from Valiant aircraft'. This had to be one of the more pointless memos sent to what must have been a very busy planning team.

The fact that Britain had recently joined the nuclear club was reinforced by two separate references in the planning documents. In the memo on 'Forces available for operations in M.E.A.F.' (and as referenced in the Cabinet meeting on 27 July) it was stated that 31 Special Weapons were available, each with a yield of 10 kilotons. In addition, on 3 August 1956, the Air Ministry produced a document on 'The feasibility of disrupting Egypt's oil supplies by bombing', which they based on the assumption 'that only conventional weapons will be used'.[17] It is sobering to see that this statement even needed to be there.

This feasibility study highlighted another difference between a 1950s bombing campaign and those undertaken today with modern munitions. Although an attack on the pipelines would have an immediate impact on Egypt's oil supplies, the estimated bombing effort was enormous: if attacked from high level it would require 730 Valiant sorties or, 750 Canberra day sorties or, 1,020 Canberra night attacks; if the attack went in at 10,000 feet or below it would take 65 Valiant sorties or 174 by Canberras. The total bomber force available at Luqa and Nicosia was only 91 Canberras and 24 Valiants and the number of bombs required was way beyond the numbers envisaged in the ferry plan. Today, this would be done by a limited number of cruise missiles or jet bombers with laser-guided precision weapons. Needless to say, the oil installations were not attacked.

5

TRAINING

For the aircrews involved in Operation Musketeer their normal squadron routine, at home in the UK, would have involved training to improve their navigation, bombing and general aircraft operation, mostly based on individual crew sorties. In addition, Bomber Command regularly staged exercises to involve multiple crews from different squadrons and bases. When this author was on Vulcan squadrons, we had Basic Training Requirements (BTRs) that all crews had to complete on a six-month basis, as well as take part in the larger exercises such as Taceval, Blue Moon, Casino Cash and Black Eagle. The BTRs were to hone individual skills; the larger exercises were to test Bomber Command's response to different scenarios. As the majority of squadrons assigned to Musketeer were based in the UK or Germany they would now need to practice navigation and bombing over a desert landscape with few ground features and even fewer navigation aids. In November 1954, in a planning conference for operations Alacrity and Tasman, it was stated that the Canberra could drop six 1,000lb bombs from between 3,000 and 25,000 feet 'to an operational accuracy of 500 yards'.[1] It is more than likely that this assessment was based on squadron BTR results against targets on live bombing ranges around the UK, such as Wainfleet. In Operation Musketeer, they would be operating largely at night, against targets for which they had poor maps and inadequate photo reconnaissance, using target indicators and Marker flares. Although operations against Egypt did not start until October 1956, the 1954 withdrawal from Suez, as well as the requirements of the Anglo-Jordanian treaty (leading to the planning for Alacrity and Tasman), meant that training which would prove useful in October 1956, started much earlier in that year.

The crews were to bomb their Egyptian targets visually, from high level with the T4 bombsight; the Second World War Lancaster crews might have felt at home on these sorties. In November 1954, and again in April 1955, tests of the T4 sight in a Canberra were carried out on the Filfla range at Malta. The target was a large rock, 100 yards long and 50 yards wide, with the approach made over the sea; attacks were carried out at 25,000, 32,000 and 40,000 feet. While these trials are useful for assessing the effectiveness of a system, they are not representative of actual targets. The result of the trial was that the T4 was considered easy to use and that for accurate bombing results the only two requirements were a fully working Green Satin and a good bombing team, which depended upon perfect understanding and cooperation between the bomb aimer and the pilot. Accurate flying and anticipation was required of the pilot on the final stages of the bomb runs; he had to anticipate changes to power settings of 400-500 rpm when the bomb doors were opened, causing increased drag. It then took approximately six seconds for him to adjust to the change and there were then some 30 seconds of the final run during which the pilot had to maintain a stable platform while the bomb aimer gave required heading changes, "Left-Left, Steady" or "Right, Steady". In a conversation with the author,[2] George Perrin (he was a Flying Officer navigator on 214 Squadron at the time) stated that the Valiants had done very little visual bombing in the period prior to Suez. As part of the requirement for the Valiant force before they were deployed all crews were required to complete at least one sortie dropping eight bombs visually from high level; not an extensive training regime.

The Filfla trial results may have been satisfactory, but they pale beside modern weaponry; the 1955 results produced a 50 percent circular error (the area within which 50 percent of bombs would be expected to fall) of 780 feet from a height of 40,000 feet at a True Air Speed (TAS) of 400 knots.[3] The plot of the bombs dropped shows that out of 93 bombs, only 12 fell within 500 feet of the target.[4] However, the conclusion was that 'reasonably skilled aircrew' using the T4 under 'good conditions' should obtain 'the required accuracy of a 50 percent circular error of 1,350 feet from a height of 50,000 feet'. It will be worth bearing this figure in mind when the post-raid reports are given in a later chapter.

TARGET ILLUMINATION AND MARKING TRIAL, MARCH 1956

As we have seen, the Canberra force relied primarily on visual bombing, which, as the name implies, requires that the target or some other aiming point, should be visible to the bomb aimer. During the Second World War, Bomber Command implemented a technique of target marking and illumination using the Pathfinder Force. In February 1956, 139 Squadron was tasked to carry out a trial and develop recommendations for a similar procedure that could be implemented by Bomber Command. [5] It should be remembered that at this point Nasser had not made his move on the Canal, but Britain was still aware of its obligations to Jordan and so would need a bombing technique that did not rely on navigation aids, such as the GEE-H (G-H) utilised in Germany.

Canberra B.Mk 6, serial WT369 of No. 139 Squadron. Notable is the Blue Shadow antenna installed low on the forward fuselage (visible beneath the front part of the engine nacelle). This jet served with No. 139 Squadron during Operation Musketeer, when the unit led many of the air raids by marking targets for other bombers – and frequently deployed a mix of Target Indicators and 1,000lb bombs. (MAP)

A row of Canberra B.Mk 2s from No. 27 Squadron, seen at RAF Nicosia. Visible second from the front is serial number WH728. Notably, all are yet to receive so-called 'Suez Stripes'. (Albert Grandolini Collection)

GEE was a navigation aid developed during the Second World War, the addition of the 'H' suffix designated the bombing system. Without going into detail, the navigator/bomb aimer was taking his position from a grid of intersecting hyperbolic lines produced by 'master' and 'slave' stations on the ground and interpreted from a CRT display in the aircraft. While this could be effective in Europe, it was of no use in the Middle East as the required stations were not available, hence the recourse to visual bombing.[6]

The trial allocated to 139 Squadron ran from 16-29 March 1956, and was based at Idris in Libya; relations between that country and the UK were friendlier than in recent years. One of the primary aims of the detachment was to 'determine the optimum illuminating height and spacing for flares and to practice marker tactics'. From that, they were to make recommendations on the tactics to be employed by a bomber force: the bombing phase of Musketeer employed the techniques developed during this trial.

Ten Canberra B.6 aircraft were allocated to the exercise, and as G-H could not be used, all were fitted with sidescan radar (Blue Shadow) as a navigation aid, but the trial showed up some of the problems that the crews would experience in October. Blue Shadow had only one, eight-foot-long aerial, mounted on the right-hand side of the aircraft, forward and below the wing root. This installation only allowed for a scan of the track on the starboard side of the aircraft and at 40,000 feet, this extended out from 5 miles to 35 miles to the right of the aircraft's track.[7] The output was not via the usual radar CRT display but came from a printer that produced a trace on heat sensitive paper; the interpretation could be difficult if there were no definite ground features. In a trial in May 1952, it was assessed as capable of 'navigation at high-level to within two to ten miles anywhere in the world'.[8] However, Blue Shadow had serviceability problems; of 60 sorties flown with the equipment, it was only operable on 21 of them. If Blue Shadow (BS) had worked reliably, and if there had been previous BS reconnaissance and identifiable responses, then the report stated that navigation and timing would have been 'well within the capability of the single navigator crew'. As it was, map reading became the primary mode of navigation because with 'the slightest haze little or no ground detail was visible to the pilot and only the navigator in the bomb aimers position was able to see the ground and give accurate positions to the plotter'.[9] The trial showed that unless Blue Shadow accuracy and reliability could be improved then it was 'essential' that the Canberra be flown as a three-man crew, and that is what the squadrons did for Musketeer, where the navigation problems over Egypt would be similar to those in Libya. George Perrin, a navigator on Valiants in 1956, made the comment to the author that the heat in the Canberra cockpit dried out the paper on which Blue Shadow printed its trace, making it difficult to use in that environment. In addition, with the delay in printing, it was best used as an aid to tell you where you had been, rather than where you were.[10]

The result of the trial was a recommendation for a pathfinder force, similar to that of the Second World War, which would lead the attacks to mark and illuminate the target. The trial suggested one marker crew and three to follow with flares, but most of the Musketeer raids used two markers (M1 and M2) and two with flares (F1 and F2). The four aircraft were to follow each other at intervals of 2-3 minutes. The Markers would put down their target indicators over the target position and then orbit to one side, a little above the flare ignition height of around 5,000 feet. From this position, they would give directions to the flare carriers so that their ordnance would illuminate the target area for the rest of the bomber stream.

As well as the Canberra, the RAF intended to deploy its latest bomber, the Vickers Valiant. In its role as Britain's nuclear deterrent the Valiant was to be equipped with the NBS system but by the time of Suez only six aircraft had this fit. To meet the requirements of Musketeer, 'they were immediately equipped with a visual bombsight similar to that used in the last war. High altitude visual bombing became the order of the day'.[11] It is worth noting that the first British nuclear weapon (Blue Danube) dropped from a Valiant on 11 October 1956, only a couple of weeks before Musketeer, was also released visually.[12]

Each Valiant raid during Musketeer was to be led by one of the NBS radar equipped aircraft, which dropped a proximity marker on the target, with the following Valiants bombing visually. The planned attacks varied depending on whether Valiants were or were not involved, but the following gives a good indication of the attack technique used. A mixed force of Valiants and Canberras was capable of releasing approximately 150 x 1,000lb HE bombs on the target, often with differing time delays for detonation depending on the type of target; runways and hardstanding required penetration, while vehicle assembly parks and aircraft required the blast effect of an explosion just above ground level.

In the following example, 'H' hour is Time on Target, TOT:

- H minus 15 minutes, target will be marked by two Valiant NBS aircraft dropping red or green Target Indicators (TIs).
- H minus 12 minutes, Marker No.1 (M1) will release 8 x 4.5 inch recce flares.
- H minus 10 minutes, M2 will release 8 x 4.5 inch recce flares.
- H minus 8 and H minus 6 minutes, Flare aircraft No.1 & 2 (F1 & F2) will each drop a further 12 flares in accordance with instructions passed by M1. [M1 remains in the area as Master Bomber].
- H minus 5, (or earlier if practicable) M1 will dive bomb one green or red TI at aiming point. [This is a Canberra manoeuvre, not one employed by the Valiants.] This will be assessed for accuracy by the marker aircraft and will be backed up by a further 2 or 3 red or green TIs. The force will then be instructed to bomb as planned.
- H to H plus 12 minutes, target bombed by main force.[13]

In spite of the marker training done by 139 Squadron, it should still be borne in mind that all the crews employed on Operation Musketeer came from squadrons whose primary role was bombing in the European theatre, using GEE-H backed up by good quality maps and photo reconnaissance. The operation against Suez was pulled together at short notice, with all information regarding Israel and the 'real' enemy being withheld until the last moment. In addition, target information was scant and navigation reduced largely to map reading with inadequate maps and photo reconnaissance. It is not surprising therefore that a few days into the bombing operations the powers that be came to the conclusion that 'The accuracy of the bombing of targets in Egypt since the outbreak of hostilities has been of an average standard when considered in relation to the conditions obtaining at the time'.[14] As a result, changes were brought in from 4 November, but by then the bombing campaign was almost over.

Up to that point, much of the bombing had been done from up to 40,000 feet and one reason for that had been the risk of opposition against the undefended bombers. However, as the anti-aircraft flak had been largely ineffective, and the EAF was remarkable by

A Valiant B.Mk 1 (probably serial WF223) accompanied by a Canberra B.Mk 2, during a training flight sometime in October 1956. The two types flew several air raids in such mixed formations during Operation Musketeer. (Albert Grandolini Collection)

Ground crew waiting while the flight crew boarded a Valiant B.Mk 1 bomber prior to the next sortie. (Albert Grandolini Collection)

between 8-10,000 feet. The Valiants on Malta, however, were restricted to operating at night and only above 25,000 feet – nobody wanted to be responsible for losing a V-bomber.

Mention has already been made of the inaccuracies of 'dumb' bombs compared to modern guided munitions, and one of the variables was the strength and direction of the wind at the bombing height. Crews based their flight planning on the winds assessed for them by the Met officer[15] on the day. During a sortie it was the navigator's job to constantly attempt to compute the actual wind at the height he was flying so that he could correct the planned wind, and so his heading and TOT. All the navigators might well arrive over the target with a different computed wind speed and direction at the release point and height in practice and as a result the bombs will not all impact at the same place. One of the comments that came up in many of the post-raid reports (we will come to the raids in a later chapter) was the need for a 'wind-finding' crew in the target area. From 4 November, selected crews were given this task and

its absence, the decision was taken to fly lower. As the Canberras flying from Malta were operating at the limit of their range there would be no change to their transit and bombing heights, but the same restriction did not apply to those based on Cyprus. While operating restrictions at Nicosia meant that returning crews were required to hold adequate fuel reserves for the recovery procedures, sorties of less than two and a half hours' duration could be flown

A front view at the cockpit of the Valiant B.Mk 1 bomber, with pilot in the left-hand seat (right of the photo) and the co-pilot on his right. (Albert Grandolini Collection)

The instrument panel of the Valiant B.Mk 1, taken from in between the ejection seats for the pilot and co-pilot. Dominating the centre of the panel are the gauges for the four engines and directly below them are the throttle levers. (Albert Grandolini Collection)

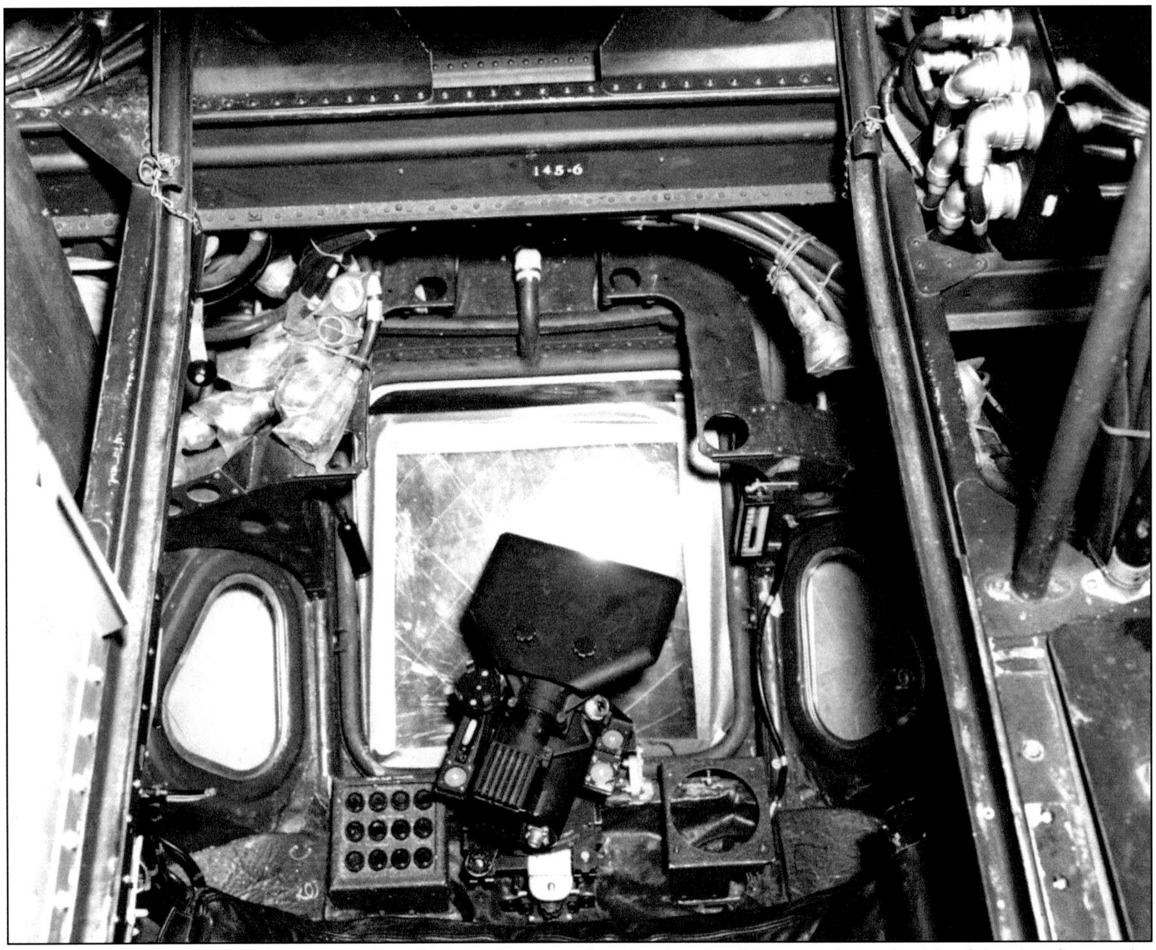

This photo shows the 'prone' position for the navigator/bomb aimer. This was below the pilots in a 'blister' on the underside of the aircraft nose. The three windows can be seen in the photo as well as the position for the visual bomb sight. (Albert Grandolini Collection)

had to broadcast the accurate bombing wind to the aircraft in the following bomber stream, as in this example: "Call-sign Breeze Leader [the wind finder], to call-sign Combine [the bomber stream]. Bombing wind is 270/25/15." This meant that the wind was from 270 degrees at 25 knots at 15,000 feet. The cease-fire came into play too soon to see if this made much difference to bombing accuracy.

There is one further innovation that was introduced in the attempt to improve the effectiveness of the bombing: offset marking. This technique involved aiming at a point other than the target and releasing the bombs after a predetermined delay. This might appear to be introducing unnecessary difficulties, but it has benefits. Exploding bombs, especially in a sandy, desert environment will create a lot of dust, haze and smoke, which can obscure the aiming point, as well as starting fires that might distract following crews from the aiming markers. With offset marking, the markers that *define the aiming point* are dropped before reaching the target, any smoke and fires from exploding bombs do not obscure the aiming point. The technique did require that all crews flew to an Initial Point (IP) about 40 miles short of the target, from which they would all then fly the same track, passing over the aiming point. The bomb aimer gave corrections to the pilot, from the T4, but using the aiming point as the target. Once the bomb sight graticule was over the aiming point, he called "now" and the navigator would count down the predetermined delay to the release point. At the end of this timed run, the bomb aimer released the bomb, or bombs. The technique called for accurate flying by the pilot and close cooperation between the navigator and bomb aimer.

Before moving to the deployment of the squadrons to the Middle East, and the operations against Egypt, there are two more points to clarify; fusing and 'stick spacing'. It is a common misconception that a bomb explodes on impact. The actual detonation is determined by the fusing option set on the bomb, which, as mentioned earlier, might be intended for cratering or for blast effect. To crater a runway, and so make it difficult for aircraft to take-off, the bomb needs to penetrate the surface for a short distance before exploding, so the fuse is set to detonate at a predetermined time after impact. Very long delay times can be set so that the bombs cause on-going disruption to the target. Some of the raids used a VT fuse; nose mounted, it had small aerials and employed radar returns to determine the bomb's height above ground. The fuse could be set for the detonation height required, depending on the nature of the target, which was normally soft-skinned and vulnerable to air-blast and shrapnel from the bomb casing.

It has already been mentioned that the Canberra could carry 6 x 1,000lb bombs, while the Valiant (capable of carrying 21) was normally loaded with 12 x 1,000lb for Musketeer. Ideally, crews would only want to make one run over the target – for their own protection, if nothing else – so the bomb aimer would only make one 'release'. At the flight planning stage the crews would have been told the 'stick spacing' to set on their bomb release system.[16] This delay, usually a fraction of a second, is the delay between the release of each bomb in the stick, after the bomb aimer has initiated the release sequence for the first bomb. This variable delay determines the spacing between each bomb impact, and so the 'stick length' of the impact of all the bombs. By varying the fusing of the bomb and the stick spacing the planners can determine the effect they want to achieve on a specific target – assuming that the bombing is accurate.

6

DEPLOYMENT FROM THE UK

The mounting of military operations, some 2,000 miles from their home base, required a great deal of planning and coordination, as the issues surrounding bomb stocks have already shown. It would also have helped those who produced the plans had they been in possession of all relevant information regarding friendly and enemy forces. In order to launch an assault on Egypt, Britain needed to move large numbers of aircraft, aircrew, ground mechanics and equipment to Malta and Cyprus, those in theatre in July 1956 were simply insufficient, and had a completely different role. The deployment of the necessary resources had to be carried out in time to be effective, but not so early that aircraft, crews and vehicles then suffered from technical and maintenance problems. In July, there was no timetable for the use of force and although the CAS stated that aircraft could be moved as soon as the Mediterranean airfields could receive them, it would actually be weeks before they left the UK.

On 30 July 1956, the CAS sent his thoughts in a signal to HQ MEAF (note: the syntax of signals is such that words are frequently omitted for brevity):

> Timings at present somewhat vague but unlikely army could be ready to carry out landing in less than five weeks. Present estimate is that air forces could be in position in about two weeks. Possibility of achieving Egyptian capitulation by air action alone or even threat of such action cannot be ruled out but position would be embarrassing if we relied on such action and it failed since there would be considerable interval before ground forces could intervene.[1]

The C-in-C responded the following day:

> In my opinion there is no likelihood that the Egyptians would capitulate on the threat of air action alone nor in my opinion are the likely targets to be cleared for attack capable of bringing about capitulation without ground and naval forces in support. [...] I suggest that we do not aim to start air operations any earlier than is necessary to ensure maximum support for operations by assault forces and that preliminary deployment of air forces should be timed accordingly.[2]

An additional factor in the timing of the deployment was the political need to make any response appear to be a result of Nasser's reaction to the Franco-British ultimatum or, as the C-in-C phrased it, 'The less warning we give to Egypt the less time she will have to organise help from iron curtain countries, and to whip up support from other Arab countries'. Given the situation in the Middle East, any overt build-up of British forces on Malta or Cyprus would be read as aggressive and so had to be done carefully. One concern was the press. Given that large force deployments were difficult to hide, was there a need to brief reporters, rather than wait for speculative stories to appear in the newspapers? The ACAS thought not. In his view, the RAF was different from the Army and Navy in that its movements took a short time and were between operational bases and that 'in our case speculation is much better than definite information'.[3] However, he did not feel that the RAF's attitude should affect that of the Admiralty or War Office, as 'the cases are quite dissimilar'.

Table 1: RAF Bomber Command Units deployed at RAF Nicosia, Cyprus

Squadron	Number and Type of Aircraft	Officer Commanding
10	8 Canberra B.Mk 2	Sqn Ldr G. Sproats
15	8 Canberra B.Mk 2	Sqn Ldr. A. R. Scott DFC
18	8 Canberra B.Mk 2	Sqn Ldr A. H. Chamberlain
27	8 Canberra B.Mk 2	Wg Cdr P. W. Helmore DFC AFC
44	8 Canberra B.Mk 2	Sqn Ldr J. W. Barling DSO DFC
61	10 Canberra B.Mk 2	Sqn Ldr N. L. Hartley
139	12 Canberra B.Mk 6	Sqn Ldr P. Mallorie AFC

Table 2: RAF Bomber Command Units deployed at RAF Luqa and RAF Hal Far, Malta

Squadron	Number and Type of Aircraft	Officer Commanding
138	8 Valiant B.Mk 1	Wg Cdr R. G. W. Oakley DSO DFC AFC DCM
148	5 Valiant B.Mk 1	Wg Cdr W. J. Burnett DSO DFC AFC
207	6 Valiant B.Mk 1	Wg Cdr D. D. Haig DSO DFC
214	5 Valiant B.Mk 1	Wg Cdr L. H. Trent VC DFC
9	7 Canberra B.Mk 6	Sqn Ldr L. G. A. Bastard
12	7 Canberra B.Mk 6	Sqn Ldr W. L Donley DFC DFM
101	8 Canberra B.Mk 6	Sqn Ldr B. Moorcroft DSO DFC
109	7 Canberra B.Mk 6	Sqn Ldr J. L Causton

If there is one thing that is constant in Operation Musketeer, it is change; the plan changed, the timing changed and even at the last minute, the targets changed. It is no surprise, then, that the timing of the implementation of the Executive Order for Alacrity (confusingly denoted as H-hour, which was also TOT for bombing raids) changed a number of times. On 9 August, the various RAF headquarters were told that H-hour was to be 0800 Zulu on 12 August, on the following day it was postponed for a minimum of 48 hours, which was further amended on 13 August. On 17 August, Alacrity was 'postponed indefinitely' and the force assigned to it 'should now revert to 96 hours notice pending further instructions'.[4]

As political moves progressed, the bomber squadrons continued with their training and bomb-ferrying duties until, in the second half of October, deployment began to the Mediterranean, 'ostensibly in support of the Anglo-Jordan Treaty'.[5] The broad timing for the move was laid out on 29 August. The move of equipment and ground personnel, which had been allocated to Transport Command, would be done under the civil charter of commercial aircraft. This reduced the timescale for making the final decision on the movement of Bomber Command aircraft and crews; it shortened it from D-22 to D-14. The following table gives the timing for deployment actions that were to be taken once the start date of Musketeer (D-Day) was set:

- D-14; Warning Order to Bomber Command to limit flying.
- D-11; Instructions to Bomber Command to cease flying.
- D-8; Start of Bomber Command redeployment.
- D-4; Completion of Bomber Command redeployment.
- D-3; Bomber forces at readiness.[6]

We will see later how this timescale was shortened, without warning, causing operational problems.

The first bomber crews to leave were from 12 Squadron (Canberras) on 22 September, with the bulk of the Canberras deploying from 22 October, together with most of the Valiants. By the start of Musketeer, the bomber force available in Malta

A line-up of Canberra B.Mk 6s from No. 12 Squadron, seen at RAF Hal Far in October 1956, all already decorated with their Suez Stripes. The second jet in the row was WH951, added to the squadron shortly before deployment to Malta. (Albert Grandolini Collection)

A line-up of Valiant B.Mk 1s from No. 214 Squadron, seen in March 1956. (Albert Grandolini Collection)

A Valiant landing at a UK base. The photo shows how large the flaps were on this aircraft, as well as the width of the tailplane. (John Dillon Collection)

and Cyprus was as shown in Tables 1 and 2.[7]

From the point of view of the individual crews, the deployment would no doubt have had an element of 'organised chaos'. Jones was due to fly out in the second wave of 44 Squadron aircraft on 23 October, only to be told there was a 24-hour delay. Apparently, some in the first wave had spoken 'quite freely to people outside the service', causing a delay for security reasons.[8] The experience of 61 Squadron was probably typical for Canberra crews leaving for Cyprus. The ground crews and their equipment left by Hastings aircraft of Transport Command on 21 October. Four of the squadron crews left the following day, night-stopping in Malta and arriving in Nicosia on 23 October. The remaining four squadron crews left on 23 October, with three of them staging through Malta and one through Istres in France. The squadron Operation Record Book (ORB) gives no reason for the routing through Istres; altogether 10 crews and eight

A Valiant on a training flight over the UK. At the bottom of the front section of the aircraft, just behind the black radome, can be seen the 'blister' with a transparent window. This is the prone position for the bomb aimer during visual bombing. The underwing fuel tanks shown on this aircraft were not fitted on Musketeer aircraft. (Albert Grandolini Collection)

A Canberra PR.Mk 7 serial WH799 of No. 13 Squadron. The jet was deployed for several reconnaissance incursions into Egyptian airspace shortly before the Suez War: ultimately, it was shot down by Gloster Meteor F.Mk 9 interceptors of the Syrian Arab Air Force, on 6 November 1956. (David Nicolle Collection)

aircraft deployed from 61 Squadron.[9] It would appear from Fred Jones' account that the average squadron 'Joe' was not kept in the loop when it came to information regarding Musketeer. According to Jones, on his arrival in Malta he was 'puzzled' to be told that they were going on to Cyprus; 'When I reported to Ops there was a signal with an itinerary, authorisation and route for us to fly to Nicosia in Cyprus. [...] We all did as instructed, took off and flew to Nicosia'.[10]

Jones' experience is backed up by the comments in the 9 Squadron ORB. During the period when they were at readiness to move at short notice they hoped that someone higher up knew what was going on:

> Naturally, at Squadron level one never knows exactly what is going on but for the next three weeks our superiors at Group and Command managed to give the impression that they were as much in the dark as we were. Order and cancellation followed each other at bewildering speed.[11]

The squadron's advance party was despatched to Luqa, but when they arrived and prepared to receive the squadron, they were told that they would now be based on the Naval Air Station at Hal Far.

Once the crews arrived in theatre, they were brought to six hours standby (which precluded 'any social activities') and, together with the ground crews, began familiarisation with the procedures they would be using during Musketeer: armourers carried out 'full bombing up practice' while aircrews concentrated on long-range cruise climb navigation, high-level visual bombing and cross-country navigation exercises.[12] Because of the large number of aircraft that would be taking-off and recovering in relatively brief periods, the crews and ground controllers had to familiarise themselves with the let-down procedure for Luqa and Nicosia. Because of the congestion and the limited ground facilities, the recovery pattern could add considerable time to the end of a sortie. In the Air Task Force Commander's report at the end of the operation, the comment was made that the lack of accurate navigation aids in theatre meant that aircraft from Malta had to be brought back to the 'overhead' to establish their position before they could be separated for landing; 'this restricted the operational radius of action of the Malta Canberra and Valiant force'.[13] In his account, Jones called this let-down 'the trombone', based on the shape of the pattern they had to fly at Nicosia; 'It took 30 minutes to fly the trombone, get on the approach heading and complete finals for landing'.

Because the Valiant was relatively new to the RAF, their deployment to Malta was preceded by Squadron Leader Bob Wilson's crew on 29 August, he had the task of establishing that the aircraft could operate from RAF Luqa. In his later account, Wilson's co-pilot, Flight Lieutenant Philip Goodall, wrote that the crew 'carried out a full load night take off', which highlighted two problems: Luqa was the only airfield on Malta with a suitable runway, which might present diversion problems, and none of the 1,000lb bombs on the island were compatible with the Valiant[14] – hence the ferry operation using the Canberras. Once all of the bomber crews were in place in Malta and Cyprus, they settled down to wait for the start of operations.

In our world of the internet and the smartphone, we have become used to instant communications wherever we happen to be in the world, but it was not always like that. In 1956, there was no internet, no GPS and no mobile phones. Communication was by landlines, very heavy wireless sets, VHF, HF and morse-code. Conscious of the limitations of the available equipment, the planners felt it was necessary that 'a communications Exercise [sic] should be held to iron out any problems';[15] the exercise was codenamed *Boathook*:

> It was foreseen that communications would not be easy when operating a mixed force of bomber aircraft, shore-based ground attack aircraft and carrier based aircraft of British and French forces, none of whom would ever have operated together or even seen the Allied Air Task Force. In addition, part of the Bomber forces were based in Malta, roughly 1,000 miles away.[16]

We will see later that communication problems almost caused an embarrassing diplomatic incident. Boathook, which took place on 26 October, demonstrated that it was taking 'over six hours for signals from Episkopi [Cyprus] to reach Bomber Wing, Malta'. While improvements were put in place, they did not prevent a complete 2-hour breakdown of the link between Cyprus and Malta on 2 November, with operational consequences.

FORCE UTILISATION

Aircraft always have been, and still are, complicated pieces of machinery with a tendency towards unserviceability unless well maintained; additionally, aircrews fall sick and suffer fatigue. Any operational planning must bear these points (as well as fuel, weapons and spares' logistics) in mind when determining a force structure. In 1954, the planning for Alacrity (the reinforcement of MEAF, but with no assumption that Egypt would be the enemy)

Due to the withdrawal of British forces from Egypt being completed only months earlier, the intelligence on the exact status of the EAF, and the number of its aircraft was not particularly precise. The situation was made even more complex by the Egyptians constructing a large number of excellent decoys; made of wood and painted in highly polished silver. Overall these were hard to distinguish from real aircraft even from only a few metres away. This MiG-15 decoy was photographed while manoeuvred into a partially destroyed hangar at an EAF base during the Suez War. (David Nicolle Collection)

As of October 1956, remaining British-made jets of the EAF – like this Gloster Meteor F.Mk 4 – were already in storage, and their crews undergoing conversion training to Soviet-made aircraft. Most Egyptian Meteor pilots were converted to Il-28 bombers because of their experience on twin-engined jets. (Albert Grandolini Collection)

Potentially the most dangerous opponents of the British bombers over Egypt were five Gloster Meteor NF.Mk 13s from No. 10 Squadron, EAF. While they were in poor condition due to the repeated delays in delivery of spares because of successive arms embargos imposed by London, at least two were still operational during the conflict, and operated by that unit's commander and his deputy. (Albert Grandolini Collection)

assumed the peacetime ratio of 1.2 aircrew per aircraft for the first week, after which it was to be increased to the wartime figure of 1.5.[17] Squadron strengths for Musketeer were maintained at around the 1.2 ratio. The planning for aircraft numbers was based on Unit Establishment (U.E.) for each squadron, this denotes the number of aircraft, although the actual airframes might change as they are damaged or replaced. For the duration of Operation Musketeer it was the responsibility of Bomber Command to maintain the 'minimum serviceable strength' of the bomber force at 75 percent of U.E.[18]

The two aircraft types employed in the bomber role, Canberras and Valiants, were different in many ways, not least the number of sorties that each airframe might be expected to fly in a day, week or month and on which the provisioning of fuel, spares and stores would be based. The air plan assumed a sortie rate for the Valiants of 4 per U.E. per week, for two weeks, a planning total of 192 sorties. Although only 24 Valiants were allocated to Musketeer, 31 were available and this could be increased to 41 by deploying aircraft and crews from the Operational Conversion Unit. The Canberra rate was considerably higher. Those based in Malta would have further to fly than those in Cyprus and the 29 aircraft had a sortie rate of 20 per U.E. per month; a total of 580 for a possible 30-day campaign. The 62 aircraft in Cyprus had a rate of 24 sorties per U.E. per month, a total of 1,488.[19]

OPERATIONS DRAW CLOSER

With the French and British governments (together with the Israelis) determined to teach Nasser a lesson, events were moving inexorably towards a military confrontation in the Eastern Mediterranean and it was important for the RAF to understand the size and composition of the EAF in the expected theatre of operations. Some of the aircraft types they would be facing were familiar to them as they had been supplied by Britain, especially the Vampires and Meteors. In addition, the arms deal struck between Nasser and Russia/Czechoslovakia had provided him with the very capable MiG-15 fighters (NATO codename Fagot) and the Il-28 (NATO codename Beagle) jet bombers. These aircraft were distributed across airfields around Cairo and the Suez Canal. The EAF was estimated to have some 290 operational and reserve aircraft, although it was believed that serviceability meant that 'not more than 175 of these' were likely to be operational.[20] In his talk to the RAF Historical Society, Air Chief Marshal Sir Denis Smallwood, who was Group Captain (Plans) for the Air Task Force, quoted the opposing forces as 540 Allied aircraft against 216 of the EAF – 110 MiGs, 14 Meteors, 44 Vampires and 48 Il-28s.[21] The intelligence available to the commanders on 30 October 1956 gave the figures listed in Table 3.[22]

The planning for the air phase assumed that the Egyptian radar systems were not particularly effective, and that daylight raids would not carry too much risk. However, that mind-set changed on 30 October. Two 'high performance' RAF reconnaissance aircraft had been intercepted and shot at, but with no damage, at altitudes of 47,000 and 35,000 feet. As a result, the Egyptian radar control organisation was reassessed as being 'at least considerably better than was anticipated'.[23] Because of this capability, Keightley recommended that attacks should start at 1500 hours on 31 October, rather than during daylight. Meanwhile, at the western end of the Mediterranean, British and French aircraft carriers sailed at dawn from Malta on 27 October on 'training exercises'; they could not be seen as pre-empting the Israeli attacks through Sinai which had not yet been launched.

Table 3: EAF ORBAT according to British Intelligence

Airfield	Aircraft type and numbers
Abu Suweir	25 Fagots
Inchas	18 Fagots
Fayid	15 Vampires & 7 Meteors
Cairo West	14 Il-28s & 1 Vampire
Cairo Almaza	4 Il-28s, 8 Fagots, 10 Vampires & some transport aircraft

7
SLIDE TOWARDS MUSKETEER

On 29 October 1956, Israeli forces invaded the Sinai, with paratroopers reinforced by armour moving from Beersheba in the Negev towards the Egyptian border. However, the secrecy of the agreement reached at Sèvres was now to cause operational problems for the Franco-British commanders, as well as allowing the Israelis to doubt the commitment of their British co-conspirators. The Israeli understanding of the agreement was that the British were to start their bombing campaign at dawn on 31 October, but Eden could not allow this to begin until after the expiration of the ultimatum, which had been delivered to the Egyptians and Israelis at 4.15 p.m. on 30 October, making 4.15 a.m. on the 31 October the earliest point at which the bombing could commence. Keightley, unaware of the collusion, did not want to start with daylight raids (we have already noted the comments on the attempted interceptions of the high-level PR aircraft), Eden used this as his excuse to delay the start of the bombing phase for a further 12 hours, until 4.15 p.m. on 31 October. The Israelis were furious at what they saw as Britain reneging on its agreement; Ben Gurion referred to the country as 'the old whore',[1] while Moshe Dayan wrote, 'they casually postpone the operation by 12 [hours] with no warning, not even an apology, the bastards'.[2] Keightley was in the unenviable position of having to direct military operations while not having all the information available to Eden, and without really knowing whose side the Israelis were on, as his signal of 31 October indicates; 'I would welcome direction at what stage or in what degree it is visualised we fight as the Allies of the Israelis'.[3] Even on 2 November, he was telling the Chiefs of Staff that he was 'completely unaware of what, if any, arrangements were in fact ever made between the French and Israeli Governments'.[4]

When the French and British governments called on the belligerent parties, Israel and Egypt, to comply with their ultimatum (delivered to those countries' representatives in London 'shortly before 4:30 pm on 30th [sic] October'), it was obvious that they did not intend Nasser to be able to accept, or they were unaware of the situation on the ground. The two sides were required to withdraw to within 10 miles of the Canal, but the front line at that time was 'between 75 and 125 miles east of the Canal'.[5] To comply with the Franco-British demands, the Egyptians would have to withdraw up to 135 miles to be on their side of the Canal, while the Israelis would *advance* between 65 and 115 miles. Before midnight on 30 October, the Israeli government replied that they would accept the requirements, if Egypt did likewise. A few hours later the Egyptians, as expected, stated that they were unable to accept the terms:

> The Prime Minister said that in these circumstances the Commander-in-Chief of the Anglo-French forces had been authorised to put into operation the approved plan for enforcing compliance with the requirements of the two Governments. At dusk that evening he would begin air operations designed to cripple the Egyptian Air Force.[6]

British bombs were to be dropped on the side attacked, not on the aggressor.

ACTIVATE MUSKETEER

With the rejection of the terms of the ultimatum, Operation Musketeer was to move to the execution phase. Given the concerns of the Israelis that their cities were vulnerable to attack by Egyptian bombers, and the possibility of Cyprus being the target for Egyptian Il-28s, the EAF was to be the focus for RAF bombing in the first days of the war. On 18 September, Keightley had outlined 'the principal immediate aims of the air operations' to the Chiefs of Staff:

> - D-8 onwards; Reconnaissance to locate the E.A.F. and obtain certain essential target information.
> - D and D+1 days; Attack and neutralisation of the E.A.F. continued if and as necessary on D+2 and thereafter.[7]

The neutralisation of the EAF required the destruction of as many aircraft as possible, but the airfields also had to be made unavailable for those aircraft to operate. Attacks against Egyptian aircraft on the ground and in the air, was primarily the role of Anglo-French fighters and ground attack aircraft (well covered in Cull's *Wings over Suez*), rather than the bombers of the RAF, whose target would be the airfields:

> The task of the bomber force will be to render the main enemy airfields unusable, thus grounding the enemy air forces. Destruction of enemy aircraft is not, therefore, the primary aim of bomber operations, but any destroyed or damaged, together with the general confusion caused will represent a useful bonus.[8]

As has been noted, the build-up phase of Musketeer had been truncated. On 28 October, a signal was received stating that 'today was D-3 and the assault on Port Said was to take place on D+6. This was the first official intimation that Operation Musketeer was to take place':

A close-up view of No. 12 Squadron's Canberra B.Mk 6 WH951 in the process of being bombed up. Notable is the clean application of the Suez Stripes (for description of the latter, see the Colour Section). (Albert Grandolini Collection)

This view from the other side shows additional details of the same bomber – and a look at one of the trolleys used to haul the bombs. (Albert Grandolini Collection)

A pre-war photograph showing a row of Valiants at an air base in the UK. Notable third in the row is the jet with serial number WZ377, which served with No. 214 Squadron during Operation Musketeer. (Albert Grandolini Collection)

> Thus instead of the ten days' notice originally planned for the operation we had only three days. [...] Moreover[,] we had arrived at D-3 without the benefit of the photographic reconnaissance which should have been taking place from D-8 onwards.[9]

As a consequence of this truncation of the warning period, the bomber wings at Nicosia and Luqa ordered all aircraft to be bombed up and, together with their crews, brought to six hours' readiness as from 0700 on 30 October. Unlike modern warplanes, which can receive target information in the air via sophisticated data links, the bomber force at Suez took rather longer to be ready for operational sorties; 'Five hours will be required for preparation by the bomber force, once the targets are allocated'.[10]

Before moving to the active phase of the bomber operations, it is worth mentioning one more instruction that was sent to Keightley, Commander-in-Chief. The point has previously been made that as the Egyptian radar system appeared to be more efficient than had been expected, bomber operations should start at dusk on 31 October, and this had been accepted by government ministers. However, the Chiefs of Staff included a rider to the ministers' agreement:

> 3. You are also to be ready to execute an attack during daylight hours October 31st by not more than six (repeat six) Canberras on an Egyptian I.L.28 base to be selected by you with view to incurring minimum loss to our aircraft.
>
> 4. *This attack will be ordered from here if Israel suffers serious air attack Wednesday* [31 October] *morning*.[11] [author's italics.]

This signal to Keightley was timed at 0145 on 31 October, before the 12 hours of the ultimatum had expired, once again demonstrating the collusion with Israel that Eden was so keen to keep under wraps.

Military operations of the nature of Musketeer require that commanders, target selectors and front line operators have accurate and up to date maps and target information; the First World War had shown the absolute necessity for aerial photo reconnaissance. Crew comments on their raid reports emphasised the impact that the failure to complete this essential task had on their bombing sorties. As the post-operation Air Task Force Commander's (ATFC) report stated for 30 October; 'Disadvantages of the lack of warning for the operation [the jump to D-3 on the night of 28/29 October] became obvious today when the Operations Reconnaissance Cell was overwhelmed with demands for photographs'.[12] Although PR flights were flown over Egyptian and Syrian airfields on 30 October, the report went on to state that 'it became obvious that J.A.R.I.C. (ME) [Joint Air Reconnaissance Centre, Middle East] could not produce photographs or interpretation in the time required'. The issue was compounded by the lack of French PR Interpreters on Cyprus, so that JARIC were doing the work for the French and British crews on the island. While additional equipment did arrive, it took time to have this operational. The workload for JARIC increased further as post-strike reconnaissance flights were required to be flown at first light after each attack for Bomb Damage Assessment (BDA) purposes. As AVM Mallorie (OC 139 Squadron during Musketeer) told his audience at the RAF Historical Society in 2008, 'Intelligence material, certainly at our level, was surprisingly sparse; we had very dim, rather foggy, pictures of airfields'.[13] On 5 October the available intelligence on the assets available to the EAF were listed as:

- MiG-15s; about 85 from Russia, of which 15 had been lost, 32 were in squadron service, but only 15 of these

Valiant B.Mk 1 serial WZ379, from No. 214 Squadron, seen parked at RAF Luqa during Operation Musketeer, waiting for the next sortie. (Albert Grandolini Collection)

appeared to be in regular use. Another 24 were being assembled at Dekeila airfield, and seven of these were believed to have flown out with wing overload fuel tanks, these were the first seen in Egypt.

- Il-28s; (these were the jet bombers that could reach Cyprus) there were 42 of these; 24 at Cairo West, 16 at Luxor and two in storage.

On 30 October, the intelligence on the EAF was updated with 'detailed photo interpretation', as shown earlier in Table 3. While photographic reconnaissance was thin on the ground, there had been some intelligence gathering of a different kind by 192 Squadron. This unit flew special 'Elint' (electronic intelligence) gathering sorties, with specially modified aircraft. In the months prior to Musketeer, the squadron had a Washington (a variant of the American B-29 which dropped the A bombs in the Second World War) based in Malta to gather information on Egyptian radars and order of battle. In a seminar for the RAF Historical Society – Cold War Intelligence Gathering – Wing Commander David Paton (OC 51 Squadron at RAF Waddington) mentioned a snippet that would have been useful to the Air Task Force for target planning: "No. 192 Squadron was able to provide signals intelligence, notably that the Egyptians regularly shut down their air defence radars just after mid-day, which will have been useful in planning operations."[14]

As the British bomber squadrons would be operating from two widely separated bases, Malta and Cyprus, the timing of their raids would need careful coordination through the timing of the various executive orders. The time used throughout was 'Zulu' time, or GMT. The timing requirements were laid out by the ATFC in a signal on 30 October,[15] for aircraft from both islands with a TOT for the first aircraft of 0001Z (one minute after midnight) and a TOT for the last aircraft of 0300Z. The TOT requirements meant that the first take-off from Malta would be 2146Z and 2310Z from Cyprus. The last take-off from Malta would be 0018Z, while the last from Cyprus would be at 0156Z. However, we have already noted that communication exercises had highlighted delays in signal traffic between the different Middle East headquarters, and these would have to be factored into the timing of the executive orders. To be sure of meeting these TOT timings, the Air Headquarters needed to receive an executive order from the UK by 1930Z, based on 'experience of signal delays [between] Malta [and] Cyprus'. The timings were also dictated by the need to have the last aircraft leaving the target area before daylight at altitude, as well as the congestion problems when despatching and recovering aircraft from the overcrowded facilities at Luqa and Nicosia. Modern communications have dulled us to the problems in the pre-smartphone age. The executive order would need to be sent from the UK six hours and 15 minutes before the TOT because:

- Signals time, UK to Cyprus; 1 hour 30 minutes
- Exec. Order and signal time, Cyprus to Malta; 2 hours 15 minutes
- Flight time to target; 2 hours 30 minutes

As an example of the slowness of communication between headquarters, the signal sent from Keightley to the Chiefs of Staff on the morning of 1 November, giving the status of the previous night's bombing raids, took four and a half hours from transmission to receipt.[16]

Not only were the ground-based communications slow, the Canberra air to air reception was 'so unreliable' that the plan had to be based on 'executive [order] to bomb being given to crews before take off'.

As the end of October approached, more pins dropped into their assigned slots: by Wednesday 24 October, the bomber operations staff were assembled at Episkopi (Cyprus), and produced an Operation Order with some pre-planned raids; at 1200 on 28 October, the ATFC assumed operational control of all aircraft allocated to Operation Musketeer; all bomber aircraft were to be bombed up and crews at six hours' readiness from 0700Z on 30 October.[17] In a move reminiscent of 6 June 1944, on 30 October all aircraft under ATFC control had black and yellow identification bands painted on them. To assist crews that might be shot down behind enemy lines, Air Task Force Directive 1/56 stipulated that on D-Day, transport aircraft should drop supplies 'at six selected points in Egypt thereby establishing caches for use by evaders'. John Foot, a co-pilot on Valiants, stated that the Royal Navy 'had provided a screen of submarines around the Nile Delta to fish us out of the water should that have proved necessary'.[18] Additionally, crew members had 'a Webley.38 revolver' and a 'gooly chit', which offered to pay 'a vast sum to anyone rescuing the holder'; luckily no one had to test the validity of these promissory notes. Fred Jones expanded on the survival aspects in his personal account:

WP204 did not see action during Operation Musketeer, but this study illustrates the type's typical appearance during the campaign. (Albert Grandolini Collection)

> We were informed of the actions required in the event of being shot down and told the locations of safe areas where assistance would be forthcoming should it be necessary. Items of survival kit were issued such as silk maps of the area, button compasses and flying suit buckles with a magnetic influence to indicate magnetic north for orientation. Extra survival rations were provided and we were told that when going on operations we would each be issued with a bag of gold sovereigns. These were to be used as bribes but they would need to be signed for and returned safely after each successful flight.[19]

Although the bomber operations staff had prepared target information for the first days of Musketeer, together with the 'force packages' to deliver them, actual targeting would be done once the operation started, taking account of actual circumstances, weather and actual (rather than expected) EAF opposition. Three targeting meetings were to be held each day at 0730, 1300 and 1600; targets for the night operations could be selected at either of the first two meetings while those for the morning of the following day would be selected at the evening conference.[20] This procedure was to allow a period of '11 hours (to Malta) and 8 hours (to Nicosia) between selection of target and time over target. This was the minimum to cover planning, transmission, briefing and aircraft preparation', very different from today's modern air forces.

To the crews on Malta and Cyprus, only a few of which might have had any experience from the Second World War, the last days of October must have been tense and a little confusing. On 26 October, the bomber wings were alerted for operations to begin at 0001Z on 31 October however, during Monday 29 October 'it appeared that operations might be required to commence earlier'. The following day the wings were told that the executive order might be given 'only one hour before take-off of the first raid'.[21] The AFTC post-operation report gives an indication of the level of confusion over when and how the whole 'show' would start, and there were 'many discussions' between the Air Ministry in London and the headquarters in theatre. It was suggested that the bombers could be launched with the possibility of either 'recalling the force once it was airborne or alternatively giving a 'go ahead' to bomb when the aircraft were nearing the target'. While both options were possible by the transmission of a W/T message to the Valiants, who would then relay the instructions to the Canberras by VHF/RT, the ATFC raised the following objections:

- In the first case, there was a risk that some Canberras might not receive the 'recall'.
- In the second, confirmation might not be received and abortive attacks would result.
- In both cases, the uncertainty would have a serious effect on crew morale.[22]

Once again, communications were a serious impediment to the flexibility of the bomber force. By the evening of 30 October, it became obvious that operations would not start shortly after midnight on 30/31 October, so the crews were stood down to 6 hours' readiness and as we have already noted in an earlier section, the timing of the ultimatum, together with Keightley's wish not to launch the first raids in daylight, dictated that the operation would not begin before dusk on 31 October.

With the balloon about to go up, it is worth restating the confusion amongst crews and commanders regarding the position of Israel, and this is well summed up in the 214 Squadron Operation Record Book (ORB), which it is worth reproducing in full:

> For the record, it is interesting to note that in spite of every endeavour, it was impossible to discover throughout the long period of standby at Marham just who the future enemy was likely to be.
>
> Crew room diplomats and students of Middle East History were of the opinion that Fighter Command and Jordan would be arraigned against Bomber Command and Israel. Other well informed crew members had little doubt that we were standing-by to assist Egypt against Israel.
>
> The looks and expressions of surprise can only be imagined when, within two hours of landing at Luqa, all crews gathered in the Bomber Wing operations briefing room for the first operational briefing and the curtains were drawn aside to reveal Egyptian airfields to be the targets.[23]

Even Group Captain Hodges, who commanded the Malta Bomber Wing, later commented that, 'We certainly didn't know up until 24 hours before operations commenced whether we were going to bomb the Egyptians or the Israelis. It was only at the eleventh hour that the plans were unveiled and we discovered that we were going to bomb the Egyptians'.[24]

The targets and H hours (TOT) that the 214 Squadron crews saw in the briefing were those in the Executive Order of 1120Z on 31 October:

- Cairo West 311615Z [in non-military terms, 1615Z on 31 October]
- Almaza 311900Z
- Kabrit 312215Z
- Abu Suweir 010130Z [0130Z on 1 November]
- Cairo Radio 010355Z [In fact, Cairo Radio was not to be part of this raid.]

At this point, it is worth noting that the information on squadron ORBs should not always be taken as gospel, they were often written out by junior officers, frequently sometime after the events described. In this case, the Flying Officer from 214 Squadron was incorrect in stating that, 'at dusk on the 30th [sic] October operations commenced', and that Almaza was attacked by a squadron crew on that date; the war did not start until the following day.

8

31 OCTOBER: EVENING, THE WAR STARTS

In spite of the withholding of the role of Israel from the Task Force commanders, the confusion of the crews as to whom their enemy was and the truncating of the D-Day schedule, the war was to go ahead. The military now had to get on with it. At 0840Z on 31 October, a signal was sent stating that D-Day for Musketeer was 31 October. The Allied Commander-in-Chief, Keightley, then ordered the air offensive 'as planned in Operation 'Musketeer' to commence with effect from 15.00Z'.[1] Bomber operations began that night, with the first aircraft planned to be on target at 1615Z, allowing the attacks to take place after daylight, and with the necessary time for the ultimatum to expire. However, as we will see, the pre-planned sorties would need to be revised once hostilities started. Although photo reconnaissance analysis resources were limited, 11 PR sorties were flown that day by French RF-84Fs and RAF Canberras. These missions showed the EAF to have about 300 front line aircraft, with probably fewer than 200 of them operational.

Table 4: EAF estimated Strength on 31 October [2]

Airfield	Aircraft type
Abu Suweir	35 MiG-15s
Kabrit	31 MiG-15s
Inchas	20 MiG-15s
Almaza	24 MiG-15s, 4 Meteors, 21 Vampires, 10 Il-28s
Fayid	9 Meteors, 12 Vampires
Cairo West	9 Vampires, 16 Il-28s
Luxor	22 Il-28s
Kasfareet	1 Meteor, 2 Vampires

The pre-planning for Musketeer included a number of Air Directives, these laid out the targets to be attacked on which days, the times on target and the 'force package' to be employed. A force package gave the details of aircraft numbers and type, the base they were operating from, the numbers of Marker and Flare aircraft, the bombing height, the bomb loads, stick interval and fusing type. Understandably, these details were subject to change on the actual raids. Air Directive 1/56, which covered the period from 0001Z until last light on D-Day, summarised the role of the bomber force:

> The Bomber Forces are to mount visual bombing attacks, with the assistance of Target Marker Forces, on airfields at Cairo West, Almaza, Kabrit and Abu Suweir and on the Cairo Radio Transmitters at Abu Zabel.[3]

Although this book limits its remit to the operations of the bomber wings on Malta and Cyprus, it should be mentioned that there were large numbers of French and British ground attack (GA) aircraft, both carrier and shore-based, that operated in a coordinated fashion with the bombers. Directive 1/56 stipulated that the carrier-borne GA sorties were limited to those EAF airfields to the west of longitude 32^0 east; those to the east of this line were for Cyprus-based GA squadrons.

FIRST RAID, CAIRO WEST

Before getting into the details of the raids flown it is worth mentioning that, while operation orders used 'Zulu' time, and crews would have used this in flight planning, squadron ORBs and individual crew logbooks frequently use local time, which can cause confusion. In addition, not all ORBs give the same level of detail for that squadron's operations, some give the name of the target for the individual sorties, some merely state 'operation as briefed'.

The first target selected for attack by the bomber force was Cairo West airfield situated about 27 miles west of the River Nile, and some 50 miles west of Cairo International Airport. The raid was to consist of a mixed force of Canberras and Valiants from Malta and Cyprus, 11 Canberras from Cyprus, with six Valiants and seven Canberras from Malta. Altogether seven different squadrons would be participating. As we will see with this and many subsequent raids, the greater distance from Luqa meant that the Malta-based sorties would have to get airborne before those from Cyprus to have the same TOT. The plan was for the target to be marked by two Canberras from 139 Squadron, with the main force delivering 147 x 1,000lb bombs from high level, using visual bombing.[4] However, as the military maxim states, 'no plan survives the first contact'. The Time on Target for this raid was 1700Z with the six Valiants from Luqa, led by Wing Commander Oakley (the Squadron Commander), taking-off at 1400. I am assuming that this was local time as it would not take 3 hours to reach Cairo and the accompanying Canberras of 109 Squadron had a take-off time of 1520, which must be 'Zulu'. The crews settled down to their en-route tasks, no doubt with some nervousness at their first sortie dropping bombs 'for real'. However, events on the ground in Egypt would lead to their recall. At 12.30 p.m., a Cabinet meeting began in Downing Street and during this the Minister of Defence told his colleagues that information had recently been received that United States citizens were being evacuated from Cairo to Alexandria during the next 12 hours, 'by a road which ran through the Cairo West airfield, which was one of the targets to be attacked [that evening]'. The meeting agreed that 'every effort should be made to postpone the attack [...] until the evacuation of these United States citizens had been carried out'.[5] As the Eisenhower government was very much against this Anglo-French expedition, which they viewed as last gasp colonialism, killing American civilians would be the last straw. However, implementing the Cabinet's decision would not be easy, as we will see.

It was now for the senior military commanders, using less than perfect communication channels, to stop the bombing of Cairo West. At 1325Z, the CAS sent a signal to the Air Officer Commanding (AOC) Malta and to Keightley: "You are not (repeat NOT) to attack CAIRO WEST airfield TONIGHT"[6]

At 1445Z, Keightley passed on the instruction that the target must not be attacked and at 1525Z MEAF signalled London that 'all possible steps to turn aircraft round [had been taken] but cannot confirm as aircraft have been in air one hour already'.[7] Keightley went on in his message to state that one of the implications of this change was that the 'failure to engage this airfield successfully could be vital to our whole operations if the Il-28s from Cairo West successfully attack our bases'. The C-in-C was not amused by this change of plan on the instructions of those in London who were basing their comments on their reading of maps:

> If this restriction is tied up with Americans movements I suggest they be told in London to avoid the road then. They could piquet with American police. You do know that a new road has been built round Cairo West airfield so that the road is no where [sic] nearer than two miles from the airfield making the chances of hitting the road much less than a map indicates.

The problem now was to get a recall message to the bomber crews, and even possibly to assign them to a new target. Hodges, who had received the message from Sir Dermot Boyle to abort the bombing run, suggested that as the routing of the Malta force was close to El Adem, with which Cyprus was in communication, they could 'give a verbal instruction by R/T in plain language to recall these aircraft to Luqa'.[8] What followed was one of those little bits of farce that so often occur in combat. The following is an account by John Foot who flew on the raid as Navigator Radar (bomb aimer) on Pilot Officer Jim Catlin's crew, 138 Squadron. Although very junior in rank, Catlin was very experienced; he had flown on the Lancaster Pathfinder force in the Second World War and was awarded a DFC. The crew received the recall message, but thought it was a 'spoof', and continued flying towards Cairo:

> Shortly afterwards our squadron commander, Wg Cdr [Wing Commander] Rupert Oakley, who was leading our 138 Squadron aircraft was told that it was not an erroneous message. This was relayed verbally by a member of the operational planning team in the air traffic control (ATC) tower at Luqa. It was Gp Capt [Group Captain] Woodroffe, our station commander at RAF Wittering, who got on the air and said "Rupert you've got to turn back". Recognising his voice OC 138 turned back and we as a squadron didn't drop our bombs. We landed back at Luqa with our load still on board.[9]

The squadron ORB shows that Foot and his crew landed back 3 hours 5 minutes after take-off, no doubt a little gingerly with 12 x 1,000lb bombs in the bomb bay. As the squadron record stated, 'After burning off fuel all aircraft brought back their bombs and landed safely'.[10]

As mentioned above, as well as preventing the bombers from attacking Cairo West, consideration was given to assigning them a new target while they were still in the air. Almaza airfield, fairly close to Cairo West was already designated as the target for the second raid that night; was it possible to reassign this to the Malta crews rather than have their trip aborted? However, the HQ staff was too late as the force had now been turned back, 'It was, therefore, impossible, once the aircraft were committed to return to base, to divert them to the alternative target'.[11] By failing to attack Cairo West, the Il-28 bombers still posed a threat to Nicosia and the airfield would have to be assigned to another raid as soon as possible. When the Valiants had been recalled to Malta it was suggested that they might be refuelled and launched for another try at Cairo West, with a TOT of 010120Z (0120Z on 1 November) but this was rejected by the Malta Bomber Wing as they were 'unable to turn round the aircraft' in that time, and it would conflict with another raid planned for 1 November.[12]

EFFECT OF RECALL ON ALMAZA RAIDS

The target planners had designated Almaza airfield as the second night raid, following that planned for Cairo West and involving aircraft from Malta and Cyprus. With the aborting of the Cairo West sorties, there was now the opportunity to launch two raids against Almaza. However, before this could be done, those 11 Canberras based on Cyprus that had been assigned to the now aborted Cairo West raid, also had to have their plans changed. Because these crews had a shorter flight time to the target area, they were to get airborne while the Malta aircraft were in the air. Unaware of the hiatus, the Nicosia crews were strapped in, ready to go, when word came of the change of target. For this raid, Flight Lieutenant John Slater of 139 Squadron was to be Marker 1, and as he prepared to taxi out from the dispersal 'there was a hammering on his aircraft door, which was opened and he was informed that his target had been changed [...] He was then told to attack Almaza, rather than Cairo West. It was just fortunate that Almaza was marked on his map'.[13] There was also the advantage that Almaza was fairly close to their intended target, Cairo West, requiring little change in the flight planning as the ATFC report outlined:

> The nearest suitable target was Almaza for which target material had been available and studied by crews for several weeks [*this statement seems a little at variance with the surprise of the crews when they were first told their targets*]. Moreover the only alteration in course necessary to achieve this was from the I.P. to target. In order to make good the same H hour all that was involved was the gaining of [90 seconds] in time (Almaza was 11 miles more distant than Cairo West from the I.P.)[14] [N.B. For more on Initial Point, refer back to Chapter 5.]

With the raid on Cairo West aborted, the first raid on Almaza opened the RAF bombing campaign. It is important to note, to avoid confusion, that there were two raids on this airfield between dusk on 31 October and dawn on 1 November. The first was carried out by Canberra crews from Cyprus who were reassigned to this target at short notice, as we have just seen. The second raid, with a TOT of 1900Z, was made up of aircraft from Malta and Cyprus.

FIRST RAID ON ALMAZA

We met John Slater as he received the news that the target had changed; as Marker 1 for this raid he was to lead off the bombers. Eleven Canberras formed this raid, all from Nicosia; two Marker crews (M1 & M2) and two Flare crews (F1 & F2) from 139 Squadron would mark the target, while seven crews (two from 10 Sqn., two from 15 Sqn., two from 44 Sqn., and one from 139

Sqn.) would each carry 6 x 1,000lb bombs. M1 and M2 carried a mixed load, each having 8 x 4.5 inch flares and 2 x 1,000lb Target Indicators (TIs); F1 and F2 each carried 12 x 4.5 inch flares. TOT was 1730Z.

Conditions en-route were good; it was a dark night with no moon, a clear sky and no ground haze. Jones, pilot of one of the two 44 Squadron aircraft, wrote that they were at 25,000 feet on a south-westerly heading and he could see out to his left a glow, which 'took the form of fireworks or something similar to sky rockets climbing up into the sky and disappearing'. He thought it might be an air raid 'but it didn't worry me as our general direction was still looking nice and dark'. This reassurance took a knock when his navigator told him that they would shortly be turning left on to 140 degrees, 'the earlier activity that had been of special interest lined up directly under our nose'.[15] It was now time for the Canberras to go into bombing mode, employing the techniques developed in the Marking trial carried out in March 1956 (see Chapter 5); the following is from Slater's post-raid report[16] and Jones' personal account.

M1 and M2 released their flares at 8,000 feet, to ignite at 3,000 feet, but Slater assessed these as an overshoot and proceeded to search for the target without flares, having informed F1 of the overshoot and to drop short of them. Slater 'then identified a blacked out airfield beneath his starboard wing, as Almaza'. Flares were then dropped over the centre of the airfield and runways, hangars and dispersals could be clearly seen. The crew of Flare 2 had three of their flares hang up – i.e. they did not release and were still on the bomb carriers. The marking was complete by H-4 (H-hour being TOT) and Slater assessed the marker force

Valiant B.Mk 1 WZ402 from No. 138 Squadron, seen parked at RAF Luqa. (Malta Aviation Museum Foundation, via Richard Caruana)

A pair of Valiants seen in close formation during a training flight over the UK in early 1956. The jet with serial number WP220, visible in the foreground, served with No. 138 Squadron during Operation Musketeer. (Albert Grandolini Collection)

Fully bombed up, this unidentified Valiant was photographed while taxying towards the main runway of RAF Luqa prior to a raid on Egypt. (Albert Grandolini Collection)

timing as 'good throughout'. Once the target was illuminated, the Markers went into a dive to drop their TIs:

> Marker 1's TIs dropped within 40 yards of centre of aiming point. Marker 2's TIs dropped on Southern end of aiming point, 150 yards distant from Marker 1's. TIs could be seen from 90 miles range by Main Force, who experienced no difficulty in tracking up and releasing on them.[17]

The bombing was not particularly effective. Of the 41 x 1,000lb bombs dropped, 50 percent 'fell within the target area, but mainly on waste ground between runways and dispersals'. The seven Canberras in the bombing role carried a total load of 42 x 1,000lb bombs, the 'missing' bomb was a hang up on a 44 Squadron aircraft. According to Slater, the crews had a tendency to undershoot the aiming point but later crews 'responded well to Marker's instructions'; they were employing the Master Bomber technique from Second World War Pathfinder operations. Slater's post-op report gave the detail necessary for the official record but Fred Jones left a more interesting narrative account:

> [The] familiar voice of the 'Master Bomber' John Slater, still on 139 Squadron, came over the R/T loud and clear calling "Tally Ho" as he dived down to mark our target. Dick Angier [Fred's bomb aimer] was now up in the nose position looking down through the bomb aimer's window and watched John's Red 'TI' (target indicators) go down. After a while, John called out on the R/T, "Bomb the Red TI, Bomb the Red TI". [...] Ray [Fred's navigator] passed Dick the latest wind speed and direction and after a little cross checking between them, Dick

Valiant B.Mk 1 serial WZ363. This was Roy Mather's aircraft throughout Musketeer. This photograph shows it crossing the threshold on landing in the UK: Mather's son believes the photograph might have been taken on return from the Suez Campaign. (Courtesy Rob Mather, via John Dillon)

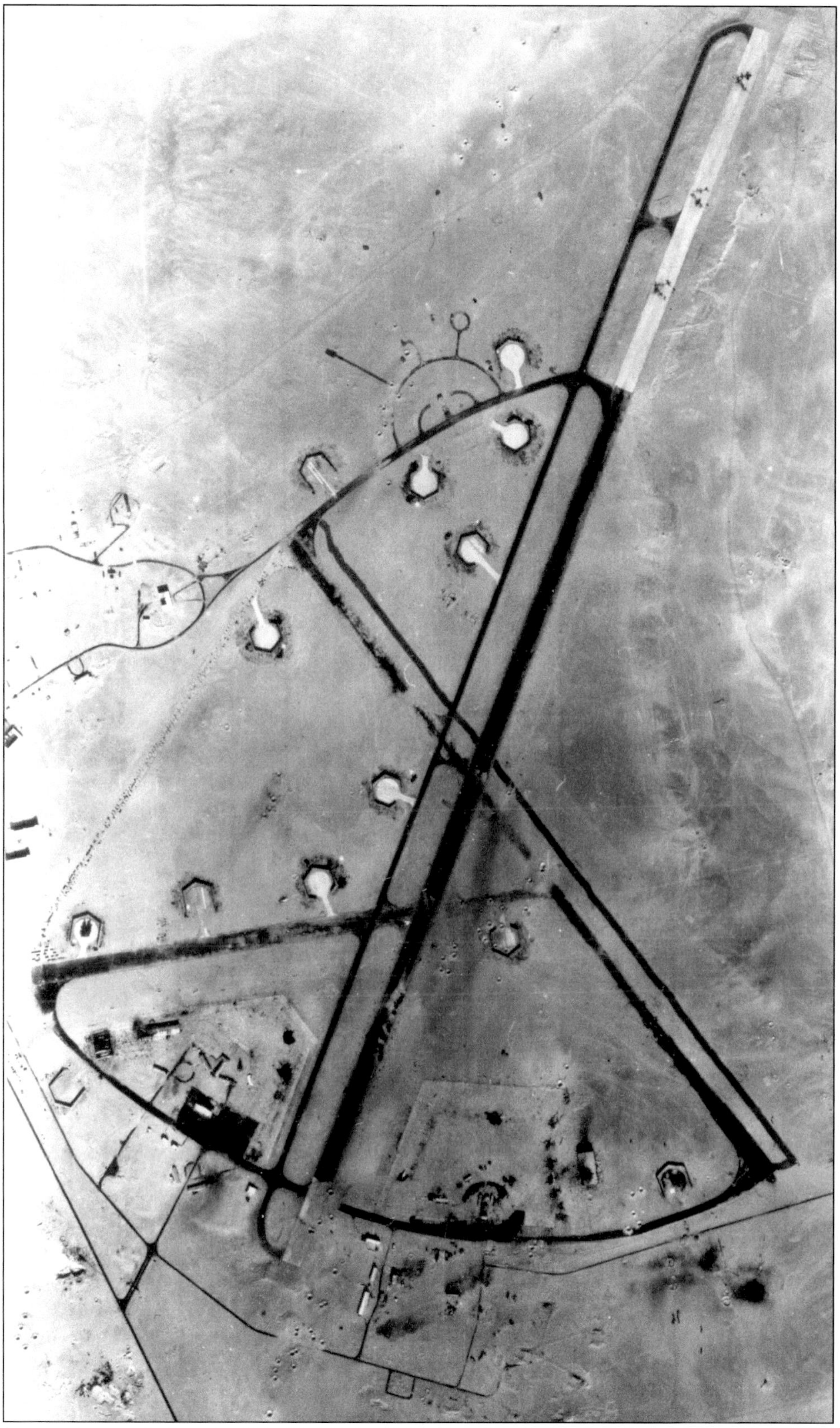

A reconnaissance photograph of Cairo West Air Base, taken by an RF-84F of the ER.4/33 Squadron of the French air force. Several rows of craters can be seen, including one at the start of the runway (left side of the photograph), one down the main runway, and two across the connection of the two old runways. (Albert Grandolini Collection)

called for the bomb doors to be opened, which I selected. We felt the rumble as they opened fully. Dick was now calling out "I've got the target, dead ahead. Steady, steady, steady. Left, left. Ste-ady, ste-ady, ste-ady. Bombs Gone". He then counted five of the bombs leaving the aircraft. "We've got a hang up!" he shouted [the 'missing' bomb mentioned above]. I told him to hang on and with all the strength that I could muster shook the aircraft around as much as I could by pushing and pulling the control column as rapidly as possible and rolling the aircraft from side to side. "It's gone," he yelled, "close the doors". I immediately turned steeply to the right and headed northwards climbing all the time. [They proceeded back to Nicosia.] We settled into a quiet routine only punctuated now and then with the statutory fuel and electrics checks and the "huff puff" oxygen check, "connected and flowing", contents, etc. We were flying back at around 30,000 feet when a light on the fuel panel came on indicating that the port fuel pump in number 3 tank had failed. Fuel was gravity fed and the engines kept going and we continued on our way home.[18]

With the approach to Nicosia, Jones' crew (like all the others) had their sortie extended by the procedures necessary because of the lack of facilities for recovering large numbers of aircraft in rapid succession. The following is also taken from his account in the 44 Squadron newsletter:

Once we were within radio range of Nicosia you could hear various aircraft checking in on the approach channel and each received an overhead time to commence their approach to let down. Soon it was our turn to report in and check our position. We flew to the overhead and turned due west maintaining our briefed height. We flew outbound for the appropriate time in the 'Trombone', as it was termed, and now that we were in the pattern it seemed a relatively long time. We then turned and let down to 20,000 feet into the overhead. We were cleared for descent to 12,000 feet at 250 knots, airbrakes out and began to turn back on the required heading towards Nicosia. In this way all the aircraft letting down should be separated by at least 3 minutes for the final approach to land. There was no cloud and we had been able to see Cyprus as a whole from a good fifty miles away. It took 30 minutes to fly the Trombone, get on the approach heading and complete finals for landing.

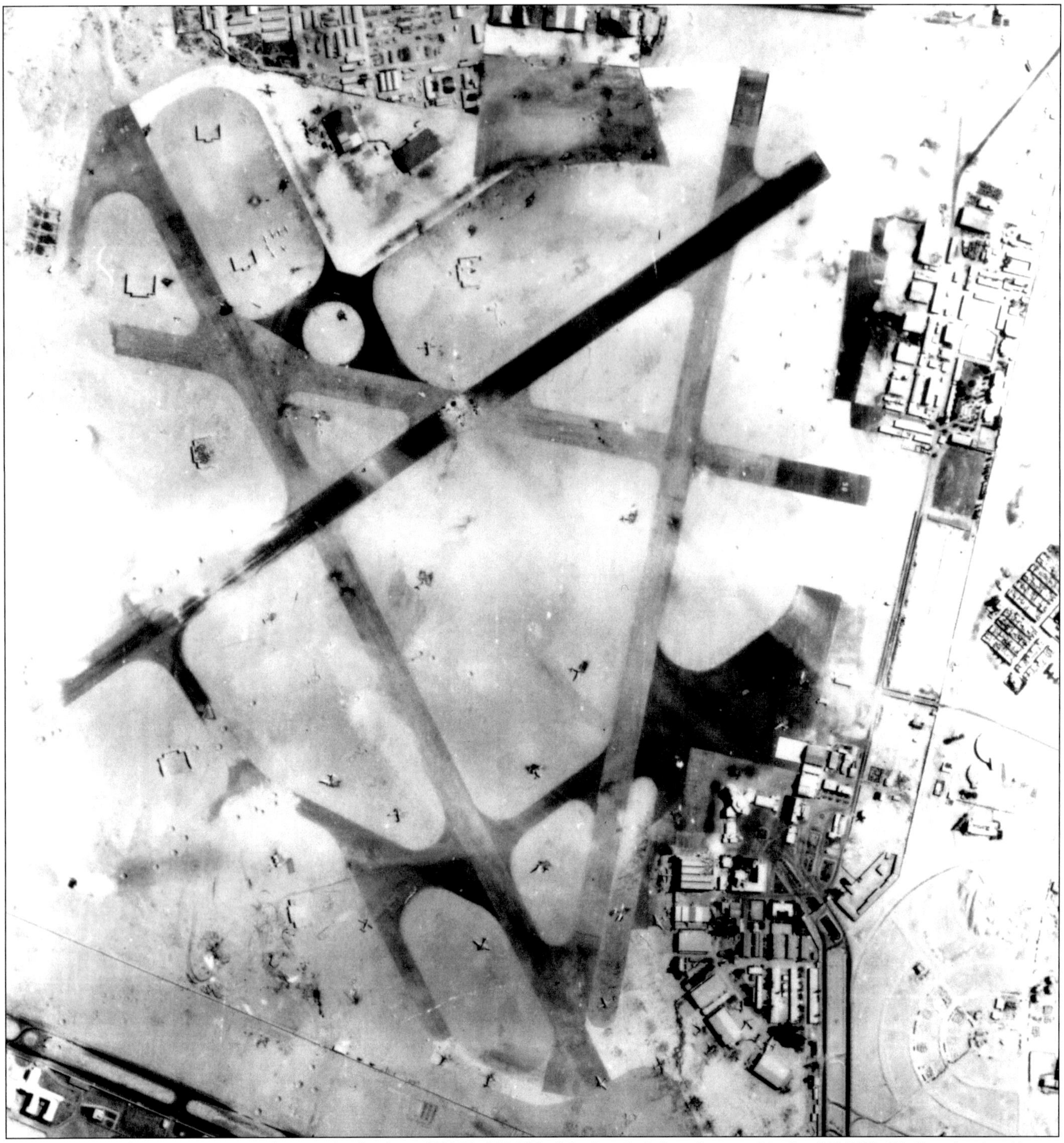

A zoom-in on another reconnaissance photograph taken by an RF-84F of ER.4/33 of the French air force from an altitude of 30,000ft, this time showing Almaza AB. Notable are multiple craters on intersections of the runways, and about half a dozen destroyed aircraft. (Albert Grandolini Collection)

The account given by Jones can be taken as representative of the end of sortie for all crews at Nicosia and Luqa, which also had limited recovery facilities. The 44 Squadron ORB records Jones' sortie as lasting 2 hours and 33 minutes, from 1732 to landing at 1955; I believe these were local times, not Zulu as the TOT was 1730Z. Interestingly, the squadron did not record these sorties as 'operations', as some did, but annotated them as 'Exercise Alacrity'.[19] Strictly, that is incorrect, as Alacrity was the code-word for the reinforcement of MEAF, not the bombing of Suez.

On their return to base, crews were debriefed and Slater's report contained some interesting comments, many of which would be repeated by other crews on later raids. While the briefing was felt to have been 'adequate', the target was changed 'ten minutes prior to take off'. As a result, there was 'insufficient time for adequate target study, and necessitated navigators working out Flight Plans in the air en route to target'.[20] Additionally, the route out 'did not take full advantage of natural geographical features' and the only navigation aids were the Nicosia beacon and visual pinpoints. Slater recommended that on future raids 'wind finding aircraft [should] be detailed in Main Force' (see section above on the March 1956, marking trial). Additionally, and the relevance of this will become clear later, 'when the target is an airfield with any other airfield in the vicinity, that photographs should be provided for the Marking Team of all the airfields in the area, and adequate time should be given for target study'. Although opposition was almost non-existent and anti-aircraft fire was 'wild and inaccurate',

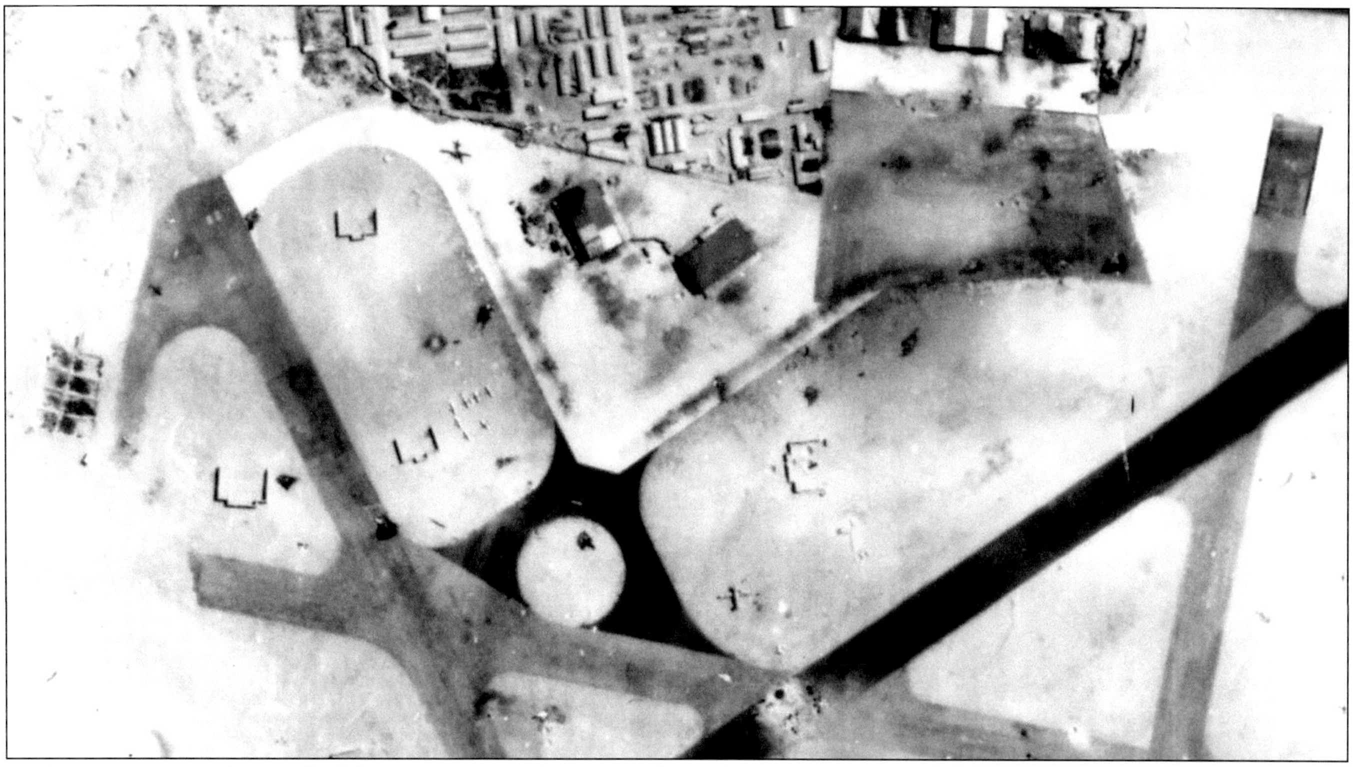

Another reconnaissance photograph of Almaza AB as seen on the morning after the first British air raid on this facility. Notable is the tarmac in the upper right corner, where most of the EAF's fleet of Curtiss C-46 transports was obliterated: the aircraft were actually waiting to embark paratroopers for a counter-drop on the Mitla Pass when hit. (Albert Grandolini Collection)

his final (slightly comic, if it were not serious) recommendation demonstrated how items could be missed when the planning was rushed: 'The choice of attack frequency left much to be desired as it was the frequency used by the airfield under attack'. Luckily, their opponent was not on top of his game.

The opening day of the operation had not gone completely to plan but, 'Having landed after the first raid and recovered from the trauma and excitement of such an event we eventually succumbed to fatigue and went to bed, albeit in daylight'.[21]

With the bombing phase of Musketeer now underway, it was the role of the bomber wings to inflict sufficient damage to Egyptian airfields to neutralise the EAF. To that end, a second raid would be flown against Almaza, with aircraft from Cyprus and Malta.

SECOND RAID ON ALMAZA

In June 1954, the Vickers Valiant (the first of Britain's V-Bombers) entered service with 230 Operational Conversion Unit (OCU) at RAF Gaydon. The aircraft was designed for high-level penetration of Soviet airspace to deliver a nuclear bomb on a strategic target. When fully operational it would be able to drop the weapon, using its Navigation Bombing System (NBS), which utilised a development of the Second World War H2S radar, to an accuracy of around 300 yards. As targets were intended to be cities and airfields this error, with a megaton weapon, would make little difference to the outcome. NBS used an analogue computer system (for those who remember the days before digital PCs) for calculating the forward throw of the weapon (depending on height, speed and the ballistics of the particular bomb) to determine the release point, while using the H2S radar for selecting the target and steering the aircraft towards it;[22] taken together, these old technologies added up to the 300-yard system error. Unfortunately, only six of the 24 Valiants deployed to Malta had NBS fitted, and this had a poor serviceability record throughout Operation Musketeer. The Valiants, like the Canberras, would have to rely on visual bombing from high level, just like their predecessors, the Lincolns and Lancasters. With the raid on Cairo West having been recalled, Wing Commander Burnett's crew (the CO of 148 Squadron) would be the first of the Valiants to attack Egypt, rather than those from 138 Squadron.

As with the aborted attack on Cairo West, this second raid on Almaza was planned as a mixed force of Valiants and Canberras from Malta and Cyprus, with six Valiants and 18 Canberras. According to the plan, the marking was to be carried out by two of the 148 Squadron Valiants and four of the 139 Squadron Canberras; it did not go to plan. Seven Canberra bombers would take part from both Luqa and Nicosia. However, there is some ambiguity in the sources over the number from Cyprus. Cull, in his table on p.189 has four from 109 Squadron and three from 12 Squadron; on pages 192-193 he has three from 109 and four from 12 Squadron, the 12 Squadron ORB[23] records three crews, each carrying only 4 x 1,000lb bombs. The ORB for 109 Squadron[24] shows three crews on this operation, with a fourth crossed out – it was entered in error as the crew names belong to a crew from 9 Squadron. Interestingly, the 9 Squadron record has no entry for the night of 31 October. Flying Officer Greethurst flew as navigator on 109 Squadron on this Almaza raid and in his account in *FlyPast* magazine, he was quite specific; 'three crews [...] were briefed for a nocturnal attack on the military airfield at Almaza'.[25] To muddy the waters a little more, 148 Squadron recorded that their Valiants flew the raid alongside four Canberras from 109 and three from 12 Squadron. This is just one of many recording tangles for the researcher to try to unravel.

The Valiants of 148 Squadron, led by their CO, took off on the 1,800 mile sortie at an All Up Weight (AUW) of 138,000lb and a take-off run of approximately 1,550 yards (these details are from the ORB). They were followed by the Canberras at 1700; the TOT for the raid was 1900Z. The Canberras from Nicosia, led by the Marker and Flare aircraft of 139 Squadron led out two from

Tractor towing trolleys with 1,000lb bombs to Canberra B.Mk 2 serial WH667 from No. 10 Squadron, at RAF Nicosia. (Albert Grandolini Collection)

10 Squadron, two from 15 and another three from 44. Although it was a dark night, with no moon, visibility was good. Given the lack of navigation aids visibility was critical, as can be judged from Squadron Leader Mallorie's report:

> The route out was planned to pick up a bend in one of the main Nile channels, to run from there to a distinctive point on the edge of the cultivated area and thence on a timed run to the target.[26]

The two leading Valiants in the stream from Malta, captained by Wing Commander Burnett and Squadron Leader Richardson, were to drop proximity markers for the Valiants and Canberras, followed by their 11 x 1,000lb bombs. However, as Squadron Leader Woods (navigator on Burnett's crew) recalled later 'neither we nor our No. 2 were able to locate the target since our radar failed';[27] the serviceability of NBS and H2S, as we have noted, was an issue throughout Musketeer. The Valiants and the Malta-based Canberras behind them, had to wait until the target was marked by the Cyprus-based Canberras of 139 Squadron, led by Mallorie. The second of the Marker Canberras failed to drop its flares 'as the bomb doors were not opened in time' – probably a crew error.

The bombing, as it would be throughout Musketeer, was of variable accuracy, especially when compared with today's modern weapons. The Valiant crews assessed theirs as falling between 800 and 300 yards from the aiming point while Mallorie judged that the first Nicosia crews were undershooting slightly, with those following becoming 'a little scattered' and with a 'general tendency to undershoot'.[28] The problem of assessing bombing accuracy is demonstrated by a couple of examples. In Cull's book, Burnett is quoted as claiming that 'All our bombs were on target', while the entry in the squadron ORB says that they 'fell 800 yards from the target indicators' and his navigator, Squadron Leader Woods, again in Cull, 'saw his bombs fall along the runway'. At night and from 30,000 feet, it would be difficult to assess the bombing accuracy. As well as the problem of trying to gauge the bomb damage from these reports, there are also discrepancies in recollections regarding the order in which the crews bombed. Woods recalled that his crew's bombs were 'followed about five seconds later by explosions from Squadron Leader Ware's Valiant',[29] but the squadron record states that Burnett dropped at 1902Z, Blomeley also at 1902, Bell at 1902 and 30 seconds, Richardson at 1903, and Ware at 1903 and 30 seconds[30] – he was the last in the stream and not five seconds after Burnett. The picture is further muddied by the comments in the ORB regarding Ware's attack, which indicates that it could not have been his aircraft's bombs that Woods observed; when Ware's bomb aimer pressed his release 'no bomb-burst was seen' and when they landed 'It was also found that one bomb had hung up and that the other eleven bombs had dropped "safe" owing to a fault in the bomb release circuit'.[31] The post-operation report by the ATFC stated that 140 bombs were dropped and all were tail fused, which would have allowed penetration of the runway with subsequent cratering; Cull's total of 104 bombs is probably a typing error.[32] The point being that sources, especially some that are recorded years later, may not always give the same picture.

On this second run to Almaza, the Egyptian opposition was a little more obvious than on the earlier raid. Mallorie's report stated that once the flares were dropped there was 'continuous light A.A. fire', but the density was 'light' and the aim was 'erratic'. However, Egyptian fighters did give the crews a bit of a scare. The 148 Squadron ORB records that Ware's Valiant came under attack, his co-pilot 'saw flashes of cannon-fire reflected in his rear-view mirror'. The captain executed a maximum rate climbing turn to leave the fighter behind him; the crew believed that the fighter was a Meteor NF13. Additionally, one Canberra was caught in a searchlight over the target but evaded successfully.

The return trip to Malta highlighted two issues for the Canberras; they were operating at the limits of their range, and the recovery procedures exacerbated their fuel state problems. Al Greethurst was the navigator on Flight Lieutenant Wilson's crew, 109 Squadron. In the article in *FlyPast,* he recalled that the jet stream that night had allowed them to make the target in two hours, 'but nearly four hours to get back', a total of six hours – the photo of his logbook shows total sortie time as 5 hours and 5 minutes, demonstrating again that memories are fickle.[33] Their situation was made worse by their 'wing-tip fuel tanks failing to

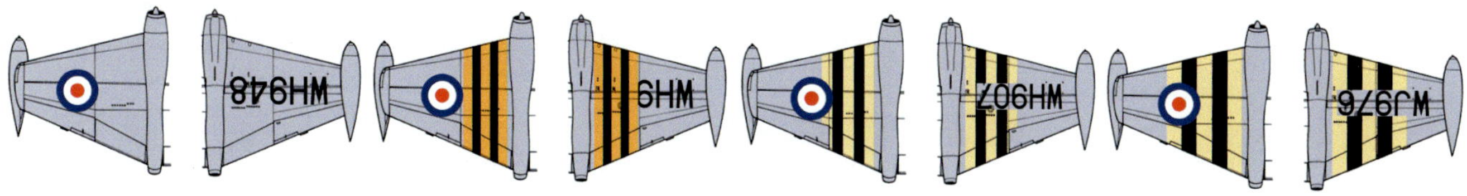

During final preparations for Operation Musketeer, the RAF issued the order for all the involved aircraft to be marked by three yellow stripes, with two black stripes in the middle. On smaller aircraft, each of these was to be 1ft (33cm) wide; on larger ones, 2ft. Only helicopters and Valiant bombers were not to be marked in this way (although the Vickers company later re-touched invasion stripes on the photograph of one of the Valiants that took part in the operation). Due to the lack of yellow paint on Cyprus, units deployed there had to improvise: most of the Canberras stationed there received 2ft wide stripes in a mix of middle stone from army depots, and golden yellow, and these were applied hastily and crudely by brush. On the contrary, Malta-based aircraft received their 'Suez Stripes' applied according to regulations. The artworks here show the styles of application of markings and Suez Stripes on top and bottom wing surfaces of aircraft in regular service (from left to right), on Malta, and two styles of application used on Cyprus-based Canberras. (Artworks by Tom Cooper)

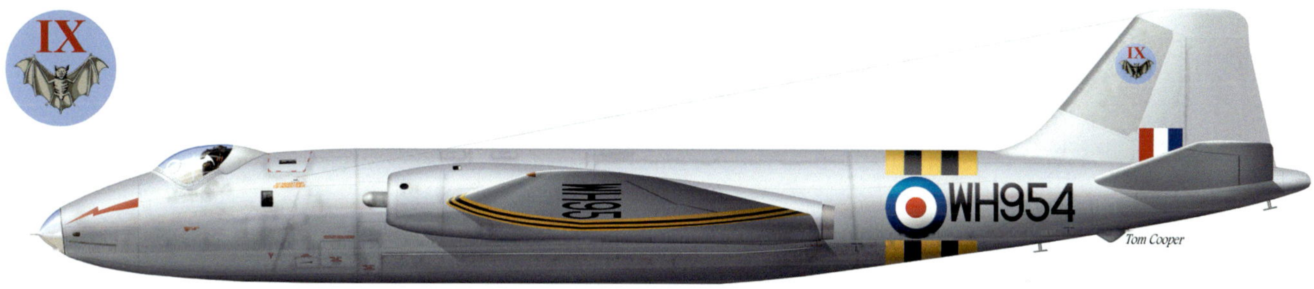

The majority of Canberra bombers involved in Operation Musketeer were the older B.Mk 2s, all of which were forward deployed on Cyprus. Canberra B.Mk 6s, which carried additional internal fuel and were powered by uprated engines, were all concentrated at Malta. Amongst the units operating the latter variant was No. 9 Squadron. Based at RAF Hal Far, this went into combat flying 10 Canberra B.Mk 6s, including WH954 (shown here), WH961, WH969, WH972, WH973, WH974, WH977, WH981, WH995 and WT205. A few received an 'anti-glare panel' in matt black in front of the cockpit; most wore the red flash on the nose, full invasion stripes and the unit insignia on the fin. (Artwork by Tom Cooper)

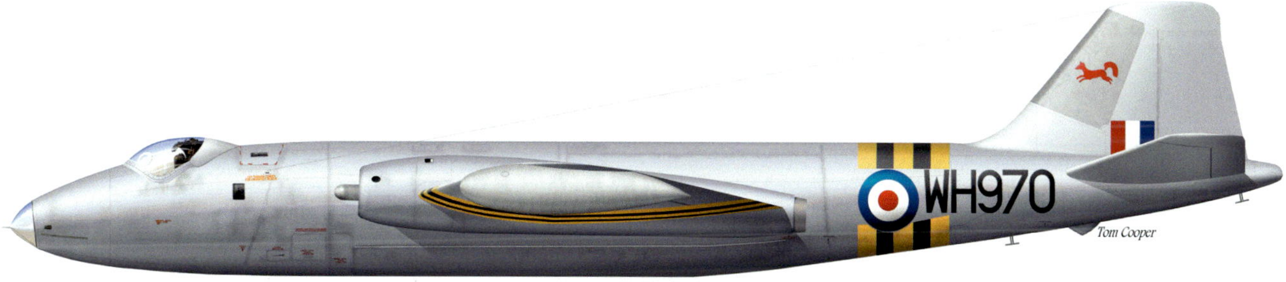

No. 12 Squadron, deployed to Hal Far, was another of the units equipped with the Canberra B.Mk 6. While there is contradiction between squadron records and pilot log books, the unit should have operated WH951, WH955, WH960, WH963, WH965, WH970 (shown here), and WH971 during Operation Musketeer. WH956 was with the squadron until 27 October 1956 but then had to be replaced by WH968 and was flown back to the UK. Unit insignia consisted of a fox applied in red. (Artwork by Tom Cooper)

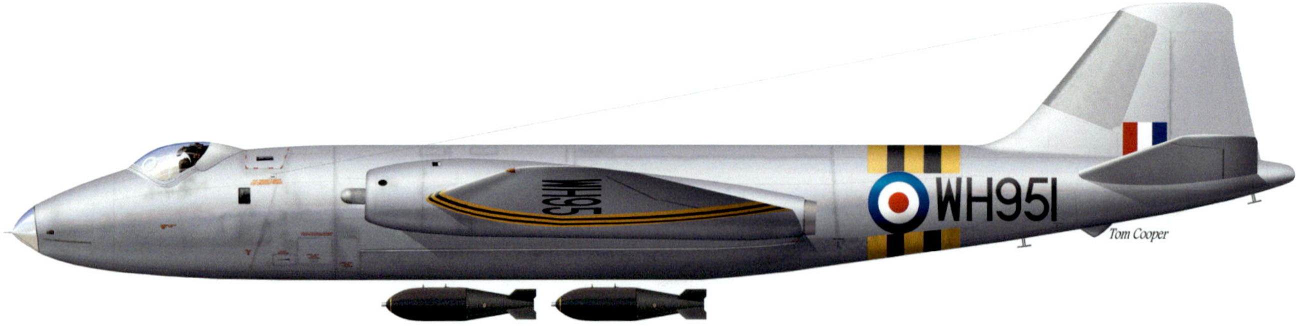

The Canberra B.Mk 6 WH951 was a late addition to No. 12 Squadron. While therefore lacking the unit insignia on the fin, it still arrived in time to receive the full set of invasion stripes. This reconstruction omits the drop tanks in order to better show the application of invasion stripes on underwing surfaces. Shown below the jet are a pair of 1,000lb (454kg) HE bombs – the heaviest weapon deployed by Canberras during the Suez War – the standard warload included two 'triplets' of such bombs. (Artwork by Tom Cooper)

No. 13 Squadron, RAF, was distinct for being withdrawn from Egypt to RAF Nicosia only in January 1956. Based on a plan to establish a wing of four bomber squadrons based on Cyprus in support of the emerging Baghdad Pact, the unit then quickly converted to Canberra PR.Mk 7s. This process was completed by the end of May and the squadron was in action soon enough, and had several of its aircraft – including the example illustrated here, serial WH801 – damaged by Egyptian interceptors. Another No. 13 Squadron Canberra PR.Mk 7, serial WH799, was shot down by Gloster Meteor F.Mk 9 interceptors of the Syrian Arab Air Force on 6 November 1956, with the loss of its navigator. (Artwork by Tom Cooper)

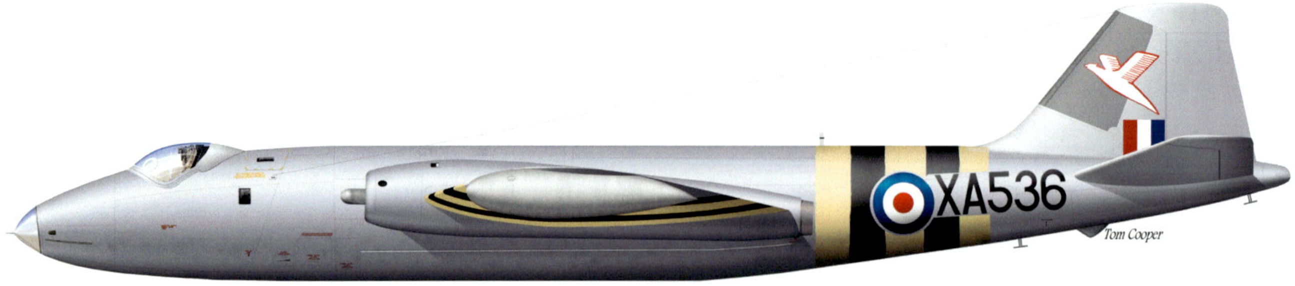

As of 1956, RAF Bomber Command had its Canberras organised into squadrons of eight aircraft each. No. 15 Squadron's complement of Canberra B.Mk 2s included serials WD951, WD961, WD980, WH724, WJ976, WK107 and WK132, all in high-speed silver overall finish, as standard for the entire Canberra-fleet of the Bomber Command of the time. The B.Mk 2 serial WF916 was also around as of October 1956, but was then replaced by the example illustrated here, XA536, which was still decorated with the insignia of the Honington Wing: a pheasant in white, usually outlined in red, though sometimes in black. (Artwork by Tom Cooper)

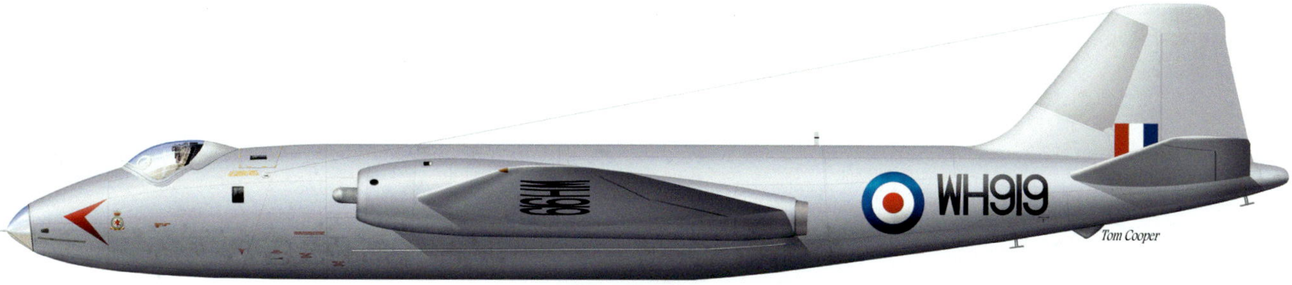

No. 18 Squadron, based at RAF Nicosia and equipped with Canberra B.Mk 2s, contributed its full complement of eight jets to Operation Musketeer, including WH919, WJ648, WJ719, WJ728, WJ733, WJ751, WJ752 and WJ753. Because no photographs of this unit's jets from the time of the Suez Crisis are available, this reconstruction of WH919 shows it as photographed at RAF Upwood in early 1956, without Suez Stripes, but wearing the red chevron on the nose, as usual for all the jets of this unit. Unit insignia was applied right behind the chevron. (Artwork by Tom Cooper)

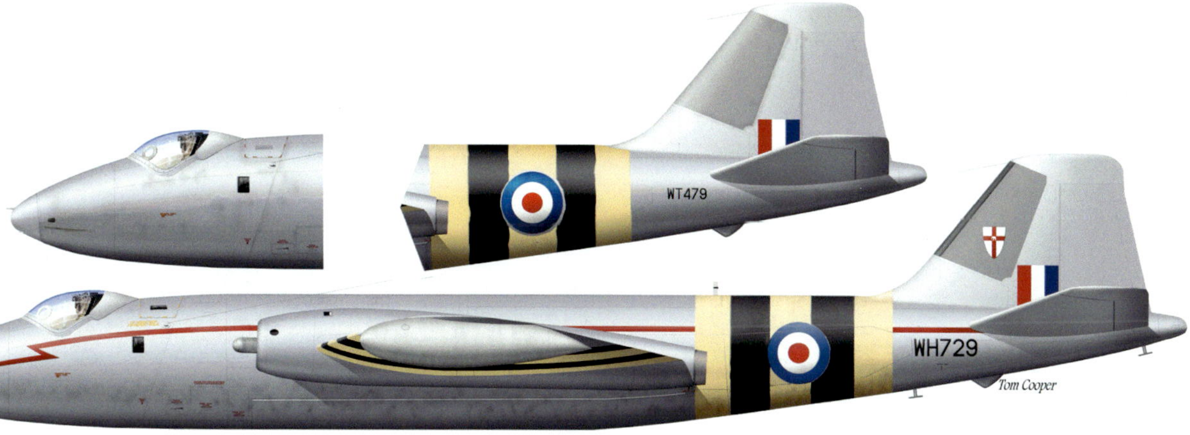

No. 27 Squadron is known to have flown Canberra B.Mk 2s with serials WH729 (shown here), HW732, WH742, WH860, WJ578, WJ604, WJ723 and WK112 during the Suez Campaign. All received the red streak down their entire fuselage, and this example had its invasion stripes applied in quite a tidy fashion. Inserts show the front and rear section of Canberra T.Mk 4 WT479, from the Upwood Station Flight, used as a high-speed courier during the Suez Campaign. (Artworks by Tom Cooper)

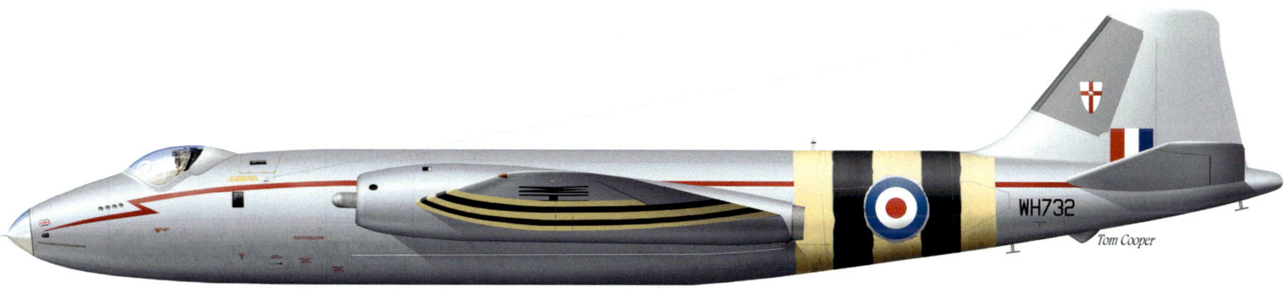

Another Canberra operated by No. 27 Squadron during the Suez War was the example with the serial WH732. As well as having a slightly smaller fin flash, and a serial applied in different fonts to the other jets of this unit, it received invasion stripes applied rather crudely with the 'yellow' colour actually consisted of a mix of white and sand paint. Notable are four mission markings applied in front of the cockpit, in the form of small black elephants. (Artwork by Tom Cooper)

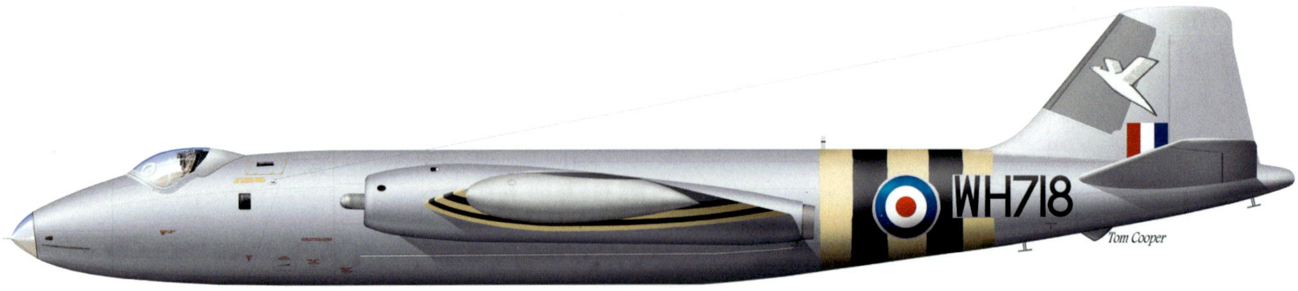

With the unit also being an element of the Honington Wing, No. 44 Squadron's Canberra B.Mk 2s were also decorated with its insignia on the fin. Sadly, the full complement of the unit during the Suez War of 1956 remains unknown: only serials WD993, WH178, WH717, WH718 (shown here), WH959 and WH967 are known. (Artwork by Tom Cooper)

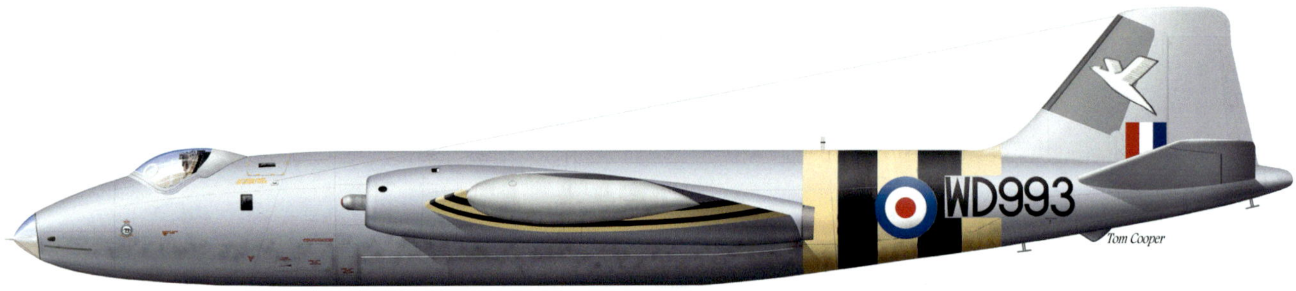

This is a reconstruction of another of No. 44 'Rhodesia' Squadron's Canberra B.Mk 2s: the jet with serial WD993, flown by Fred Jones in air strikes on Almaza (on 31 October 1956), Cairo West (1 November), Luxor (2 November), and Almaza again (3 November). The aircraft is shown with the white pheasant of the Honington Wing on the fin, the unit crest below the cockpit on the forward fuselage, and relatively tidy Suez Stripes. (Artwork by Tom Cooper)

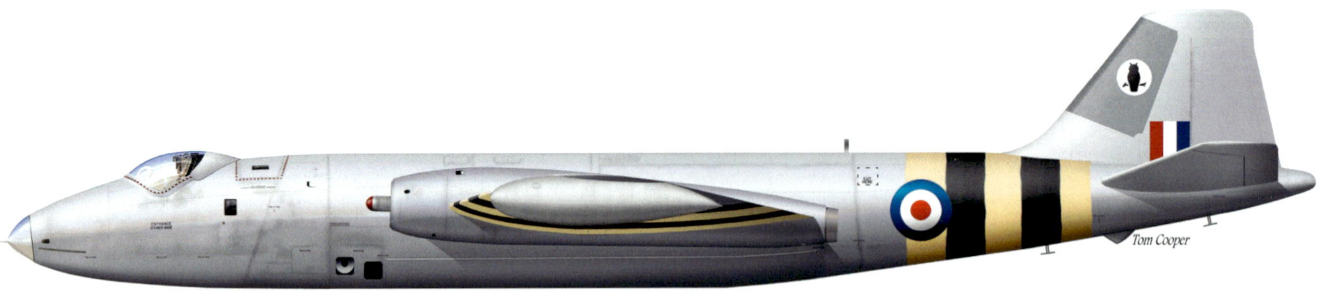

The second unit equipped with Canberra PR.Mk 7 reconnaissance-bombers and involved in the Suez War of 1956 was No. 59 Squadron. In addition to the unit insignia on the fin, this example has its invasion stripes further down the rear fuselage, and thus only partially around the roundel. (Artwork by Tom Cooper)

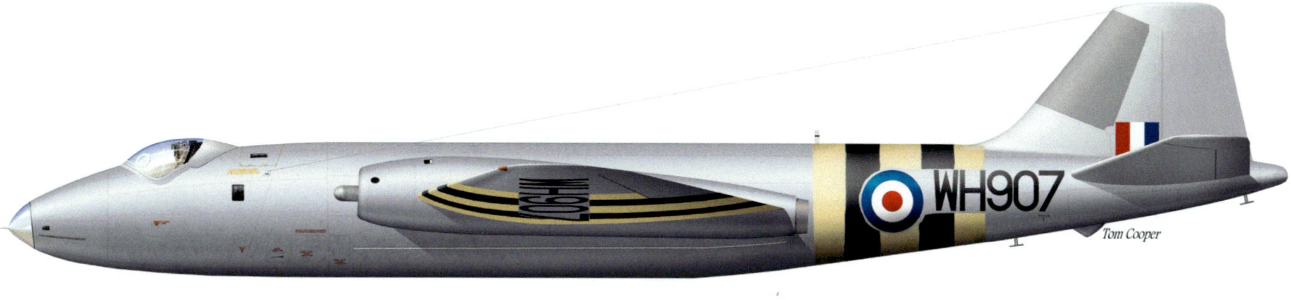

No. 61 Squadron also flew Canberra B.Mk 2s from Cyprus, and was slightly expanded to a total of 10 jets during the Suez Campaign, including: WH724, WH740, WH907 (shown here), WH908, WH910, WH915, WH918, WJ636, WJ642 and WJ647. Due to the shortage of the 'yellow' colour, its aircraft received partial – and slightly narrower – invasion stripes on the rear fuselage and wings. (Artwork by Tom Cooper)

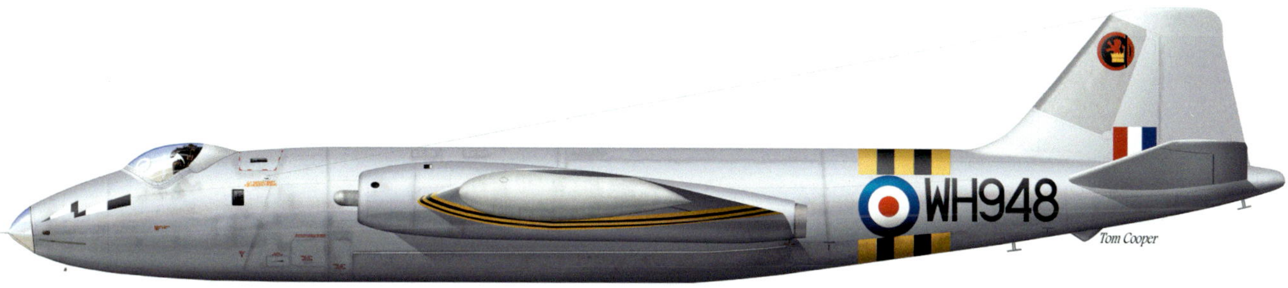

Home-based at RAF Binbrook, No. 101 Squadron, RAF, was one of few units already equipped with the improved and longer-ranged Canberra B.Mk 6s during the Suez Crisis. Correspondingly, its aircraft were forward deployed at RAF Hal Far on Malta for Operation Musketeer. Its complement included examples with serials WH945, WH948 (shown here), WJ756, WJ758, WJ760, WJ761, WJ762 and WJ764. All have the streak in black and white on the nose, and the unit insignia on the fin. (Artwork by Tom Cooper)

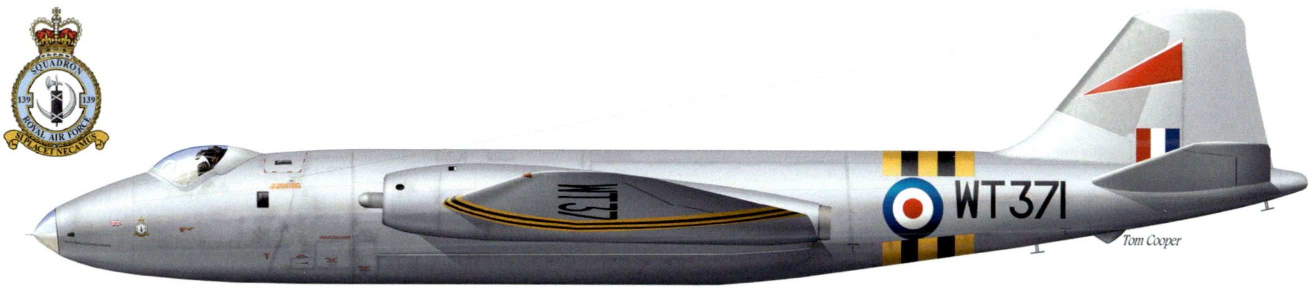

Thanks to their red and white chevrons applied on the fin, No. 139 Squadron's Canberra B.Mk 6s were some of the more colourful of this war. The unit reportedly operated 12 jets during the campaign, including: WJ767, WJ768, WJ773, WJ774, WJ776, WJ778, WT302, WT306, WT369, WT370, WT371 and WT372. This squadron's aircraft were unique for being equipped with the Blue Shadow sideways-looking radar: this provided the navigator with a print-out of radar returns at 90 degrees to the right of the aircraft up to a distance of about 60 miles (depending on the flight altitude). Commanded by Squadron Leader Terry Kearns, No. 139 flew many of the target marking missions, in which its crews usually released their flare bombs from a 30° dive. (Artwork by Tom Cooper)

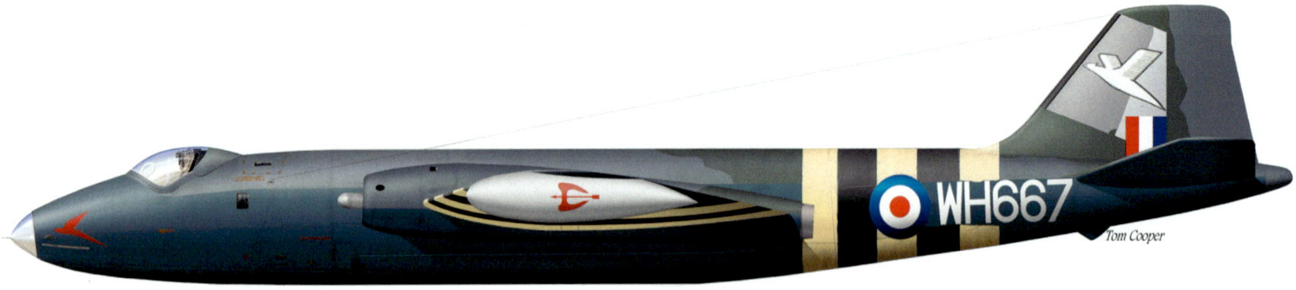

The only RAF bombers reliably confirmed as having worn camouflage colours during the Suez War were Canberra B.Mk 2s of No. 10 Squadron, from the Honington Wing. Colours used were medium sea grey and light slate grey on top surfaces, and PRU blue on sides and undersurfaces. Drop tanks were left in their aluminium overall and were usually decorated with the squadron insignia. The unit deployed to RAF Nicosia with a full complement of eight jets, including WH640, WH646, WH665, WH667, WH668, WH672, WH853, WJ973 and WJ518. (Artwork by Tom Cooper)

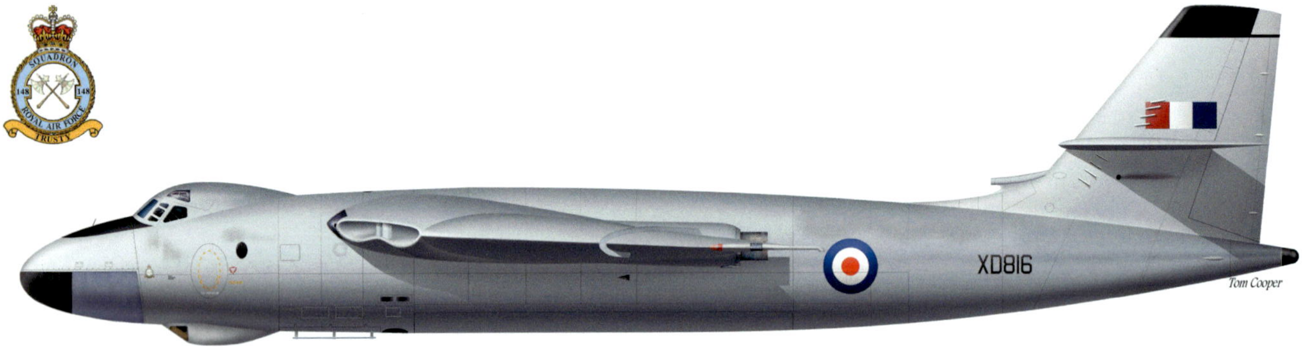

Nominally at least, Valiant B.Mk 1s of RAF Bomber Command were organised into squadrons of six aircraft each. With four squadrons becoming involved in Operation Musketeer, a total of 24 jets were deployed with the Malta Bomber Wing. However, No. 138 Squadron actually operated eight aircraft (including WP215, WP220, WZ363, WZ384, WZ389, WZ400, WZ401, and WZ402), while two other units had five each. One of the latter was No. 148 Squadron, to which this Valiant was assigned (together with XD814, XD815, XD816, XD817 and XD819).

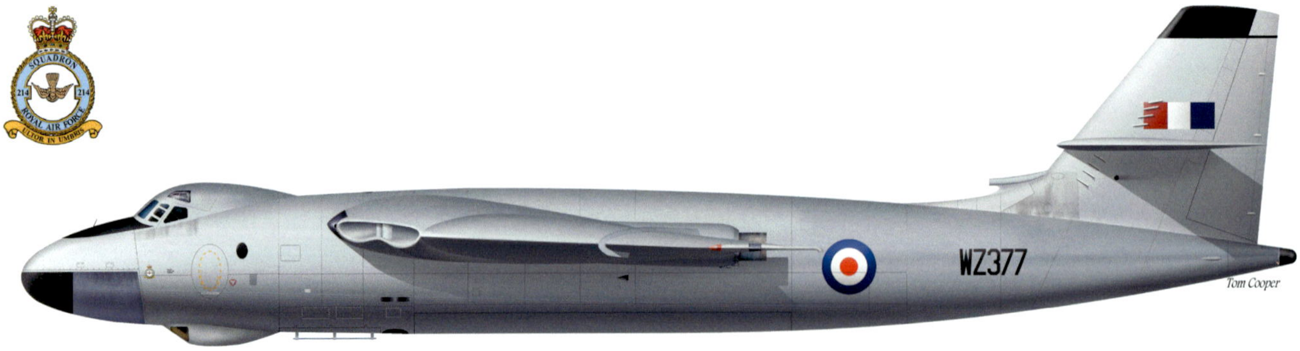

No. 214 Squadron was the other unit with the slightly reduced complement of five jets, including WZ377 (shown here), WZ379, WZ393, WZ395 and WZ397. Like all early Valiant B.Mk 1s, they all received the high-speed silver finish, and wore no other insignia than the squadron crest, warning stencils and national markings. The fourth of the Valiant squadrons, No. 207, included jets with serials WP219, WZ403, WZ404, WZ405, XD812 and XD813. (Artwork by Tom Cooper)

The principal opponent – and target – of the RAF bombers during the Suez War of 1956 was the MiG-15bis, 80 of which were delivered to Egypt in 1955 (followed by 45 examples earmarked for Syria, but only partially assembled and not flown during the conflict). Slightly over 60 were operational with three units during the campaign. All of these were painted in two layers of clear lacquer, mixed with 10 percent and 5 percent aluminium powder, respectively. They wore the roundels in six positions, fin-flashes, two black identification stripes around the rear fuselage and three around their wing-tips, and black serials in the range 19xx. (Artwork by Tom Cooper)

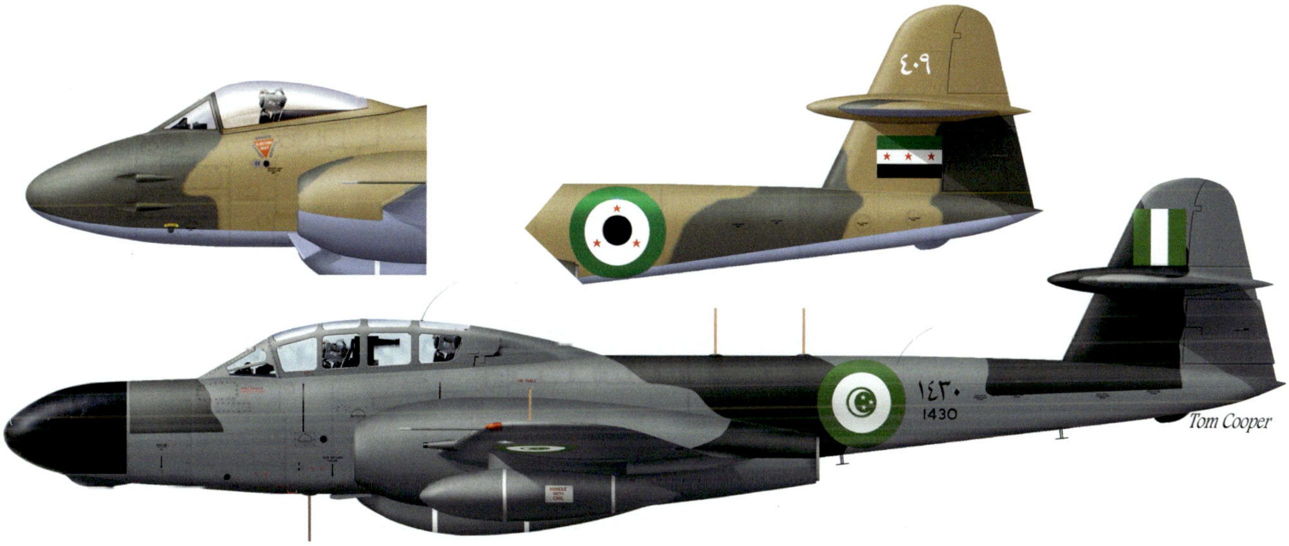

Ironically, one of the most dangerous opponents for British bombers during the Suez Crisis/War of 1956 became No. 10 Squadron, EAF, equipped with Gloster Meteor NF.Mk 13 interceptors originally obtained from Britain. The inset shows the front and rear section of one of the Syrian-operated Meteor F.Mk 9 single-seaters: they eventually scored the only kill against RAF bombers during the campaign, when they shot down a Canberra PR.Mk 7 on 6 November 1956. (Artwork by Tom Cooper)

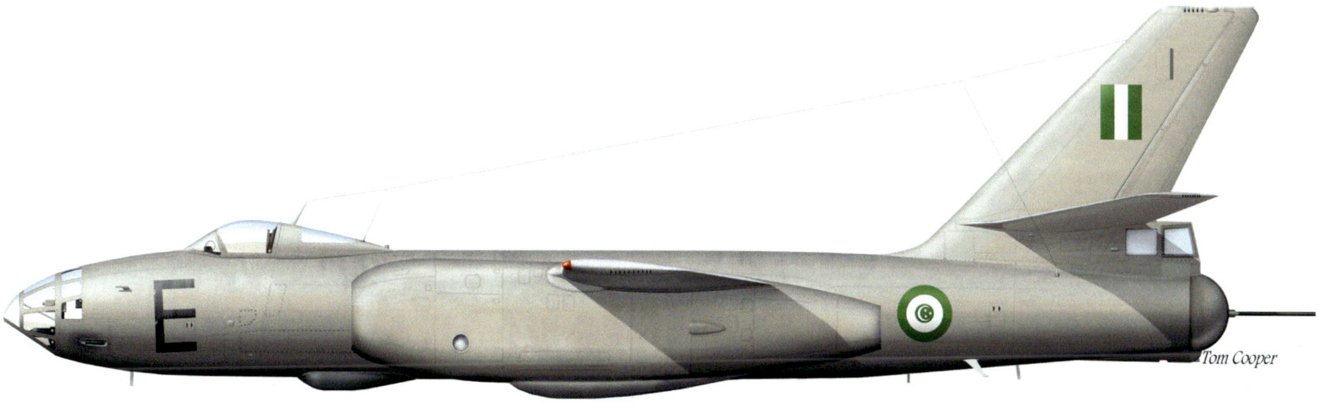

One of the principal targets of RAF Bomber Command's air raids on Egypt was the EAF's fleet of 40 Ilyushin Il-28 bombers. All were painted in the same fashion as the MiG-15s and wore the same set of national insignia. Instead of serials, they received large letter codes on the front fuselage, from A to Z. Unofficial Egyptian sources have confirmed the loss of several Il-28s, prepared for a nocturnal raid on Israeli air bases, during the RAF strike on Cairo West AB late on 31 October 1956. This example survived not only the strike on that base but also subsequent attacks on Luxor airport and was eventually evacuated to Saudi Arabia. (Artwork by Tom Cooper)

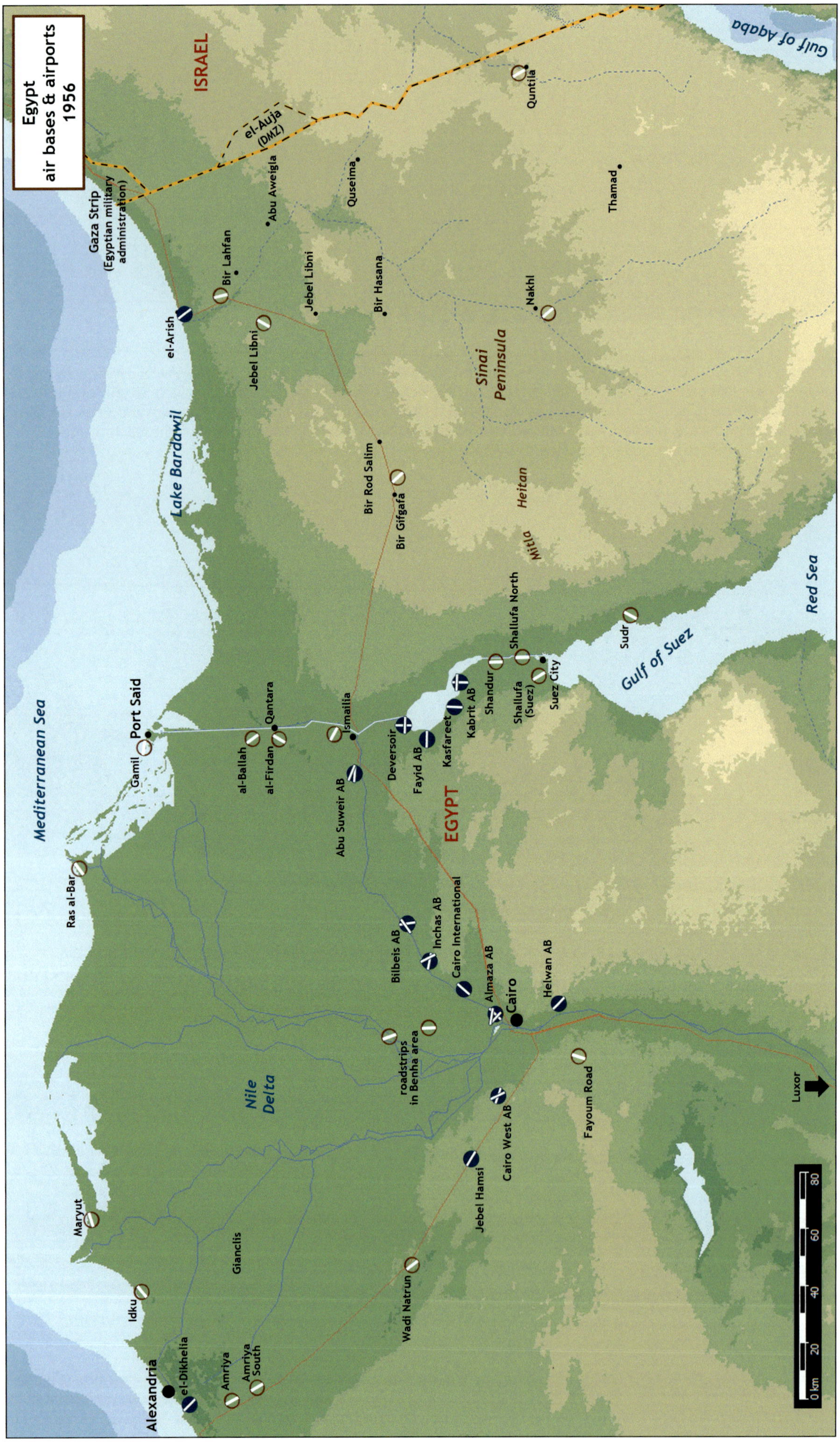
Egypt
air bases & airports
1956
ISRAEL
el-Auja
(DMZ)
Gaza Strip
(Egyptian military
administration)
Abu Aweigla
Quseima
Quntila
Gulf of Aqaba
Thamad
Bir Lahfan
el-Arish
Jebel Libni
Bir Hasana
Nakhl
Sinai
Peninsula
Lake Bardawil
Bir Rod Salim
Bir Gifgafa
Heitan
Mitla
Mediterranean Sea
Port Said
Gamil
Qantara
al-Ballah
al-Firdan
Ismailia
Abu Suweir AB
Deversoir
Fayid AB
Kasfareet
Kabrit AB
Shandur
Shallufa North
Shallufa
(Suez)
Suez City
Sudr
Gulf of Suez
Red Sea
EGYPT
Ras al-Bar
Inchas AB
Bilbeis AB
Cairo International
Almaza AB
Cairo
Helwan AB
roadstrips
in Benha area
Nile
Delta
Cairo West AB
Fayoum Road
Luxor
Jebel Hamsi
Maryut
Gianclis
Wadi Natrun
Idku
Alexandria
el-Dikheila
Amriya
Amriya
South
0 km
20
40
60
80

Valiant B.Mk 1 serial WZ405 from No. 207 Squadron at RAF Luqa. (Albert Grandolini Collection)

WZ403, another of No. 207 Squadron's Valiants, seen with its bomb bay open, waiting to be armed. (Albert Grandolini Collection)

A starboard view of the same bomber, seen shortly after the bombing up process was concluded. (Albert Grandolini Collection)

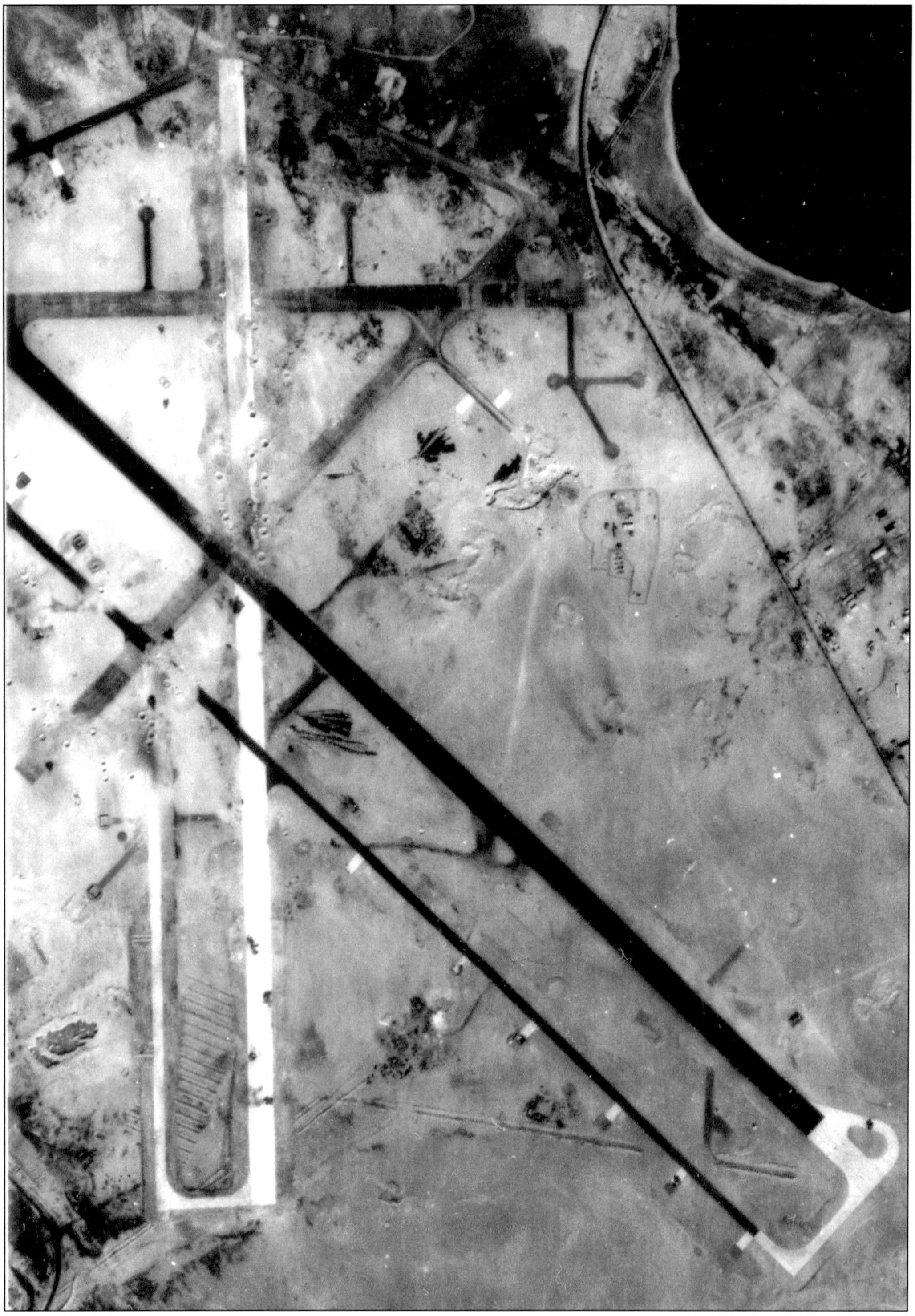

A reconnaissance photograph taken by an RF-84F of the French air force on the morning after the first raid, showing nearly three dozen craters along the disused runway of Kabrit AB and numerous hits on other facilities. (Albert Grandolini Collection)

BOMBING CAIRO INTERNATIONAL IN ERROR

Before leaving the bomber operations of 31 October a few words are necessary regarding Cairo International. Bombs were dropped on this airfield, in error, but it should be stated that it lies only about half a mile to a mile, north-east of Almaza (as can be seen on online maps). The official records are ambiguous regarding this bombing error. Probably the best book written on the Suez Crisis is that by Keith Kyle but his reference to the incident is not clear. He refers to the short notice given to the crews who flew the first Almaza raid (in place of that on Cairo West), the close proximity of Cairo International to Almaza and the fact that the crews were allowed little time for target preparation. However, his statement that 'In the end, going for Almaza, they hit Cairo International',[35] with no mention of the crews who did bomb the correct target, leaves the reader with the impression that the whole raid attacked Cairo International. Barnett's ATFC report states that 'during one of the attacks on Almaza, a number of bombs fell on Cairo International Airport'.[36] Flight Lieutenant Slater was M1 for the first raid and his report makes no mention of Cairo International. However, he does state that the first flares were an 'overshoot' and that he then identified Almaza under his starboard wing (see earlier details of the first raid on Almaza).[37] There is no mention of crews bombing the wrong target, although he recommends that crews on future sorties have details of all airfields in the vicinity of their assigned target.

feed' and so, short on fuel, Wilson requested an immediate landing; air traffic at Luqa refused, at which point the pilot swore and told them that he was going in anyway. They were saved the need to overrule the controllers at Luqa by those at the neighbouring naval airfield at Hal Far who gave them permission to land there. According to Greethurst, no sooner had they landed than 'one of the engines began to wind down, out of fuel,' no doubt they enjoyed a good night in the Navy Officers' Mess. They returned the following morning on a short 10-minute flight, although the ORB incorrectly dates this as taking place on 31 October, instead of 1 November.[34] The official records are riddled with small errors.

For the second attack on Almaza, Squadron Leader Mallorie was M1 and again his report makes no mention of crews bombing the wrong target. He does however, mention that the first flares were dropped over Heliopolis but 'Identification was wrong and Cairo International was marked'. The TIs, which the following bombers would use as their aiming point, were 'estimated to be in the right position on the Eastern hardstanding [of Almaza]'.[38] Following the raids, PR sorties were flown to provide Bomb Damage Assessment (BDA) and this showed that 'both Almaza and Cairo International airfields had been attacked, but it is not certain which raid went astray'.[39] The author leaves the reader to decide which of the two raids hit Cairo International in error.

KABRIT AIRFIELD

The night of 31 October, and the early hours of 1 November, was a busy period for the bomber wings as they attempted to degrade the operational effectiveness of the EAF. It was important to hit Egyptian airfields early in Musketeer, especially to minimise the threat that the Il-28s posed to Nicosia. The third of the targets selected for the first night was the airfield at Kabrit, which lay at the southern end of the Great Bitter Lake. Once again, the bomber wings at Cyprus and Malta were to put up crews for this raid; Nicosia provided four Marker Canberras from 18 Squadron as well as seven bombers, two from 10 and 44 squadrons and three from 15 Squadron. Malta provided five Valiants from 207 Squadron with 12 x 1,000lb bombs, and seven Canberra bombers from 101 Squadron, each of which carried 4 x 1,000lb bombs. Although they were taking-off in the same stream for a coordinated attack, the ORBs for these two squadrons have wildly different take-off times, 207 starts at 1950,[40] while 101 states that they started at 2105.[41] Landing times show that both aircraft types had sortie lengths of approximately 5.5 hours. Once again, we see inconsistency in the recording of times in squadron ORBs.

A post-strike reconnaissance photograph of Abu Suweir AB, taken by an RF-84F of the French air force. Except for few craters on the second of the famous 'eights' along the taxiway (right side of the photograph), no other damage is discernible. (Albert Grandolini Collection)

The account of the raid in the 101 Squadron ORB is given in considerable detail and worth reproducing in full. These crews were based at Hal Far rather than Luqa:

> The aircraft cruise climbed to the force R.V. [rendezvous] point where they maintained the height achieved for the bombing run. The bombing height varied from 41,000 to 44,000 feet. The target was marked initially by a green proximity marker dropped by radar from a Valiant aircraft, followed by flares and red target indicators dropped visually at low level by Canberra aircraft from Cyprus. Although the target was covered by ¼ to ⅜ of low cloud, [cloud cover is traditionally measured in 'eighths'] the indicators were visible at a range of 100 n.m. The bomb load consisted of four 1000lb Mk. XI M.C. bombs [dumb, iron bombs] dropped at a stick spacing of 0.12 seconds. The first bomb

A post-Suez Campaign photograph showing the underside of a Valiant, including underwing tanks and the bomb aimer's 'blister' under the nose. (John Dillon Collection)

of each stick carried a time delay of ½ to 12 hours, while the rest had a delay of 0.14 seconds to achieve penetration.[42]

The delay of 0.14 seconds for penetration would have achieved cratering while the delay on the first bomb of each stick was presumably to deter Egyptian work groups from trying to repair the runways and hard standings. The Master Bomber stated that all the bombs observed were within the airfield area, while the AFTC report recorded 118 bombs dropped and that all of them were 'estimated within 450 yards of markers'. Like almost all other raids, opposition was light and anti-aircraft fire was ineffective. One aircraft, flown by Flight Lieutenant Ward, had a hang up, which then fell onto the bomb doors when they were closed. However, 'it fell away when they were opened again causing minor damage to the doors'. The crew must have been relieved, as a loose bomb on the doors would have caused some buttock clenching on landing.

ABU SUWEIR AIRFIELD

The fourth raid to be launched, and the third to bomb, was another joint effort by Malta and Cyprus, this time against the airfield at Abu Suweir, which lies about 12-13 miles east of Ismailia; TOT for the raid was 010130Z. Like so many of the other airfield targets during Musketeer, this was an old RAF airfield from the Second World War. It had two runways; one was east-west, the other north-west to south-east. The bomber wing on Malta launched four Valiants and eight Canberras: two of the Valiants were Markers from 138 Squadron (their load consisted of proximity markers and 11 x 1,000lb bombs); the other two were from 214 Squadron and carried the full load of 12 x 1,000lb bombs. Seven of the Canberras were from 9 Squadron, with just one from 109, all carrying 4 x 1,000lb bombs. The Cyprus force was a mix of crews from five of the squadrons: 18 Squadron provided four markers with the bombers coming from 10 Squadron (two), 15 Squadron (one), 44 Squadron (one) and two from 61 Squadron. The crews were briefed to bomb the runways, to avoid the camp areas and were not to jettison any bombs in a 'live' state 'in case Egyptian casualties were caused'[43] – presumably, this referred to Egyptian civilians, not military personnel.

Two crews, one from Malta (Flight Lieutenant Stonham from 9 Squadron) and one from Cyprus (Flying Officer Price from 61 Squadron) had to turn back after take-off, both with undercarriage retraction problems. As the remaining crews approached Egypt, the co-pilot in the lead Valiant recalled that, 'all looked peaceful. The lights in the towns and cities were glimmering below'.[44] They continued to the target and dropped their red proximity marker from 42,000 feet before waiting for the Canberras from 138 Squadron to come in and drop their TIs. The bomber stream then received the instruction from M1, 'bomb on the green marker'. Egyptian opposition, fighters and anti-aircraft fire, was assessed by 138 Squadron crews as non-existent; the bombing and marking were judged by them to have been 'extremely accurate'.[45] The ATFC report was a little more guarded stating only that all bombs fell 'within the target area'. All crews then had an uneventful trip home with the Cyprus aircraft having a sortie length of around three hours, while those from Malta had a round trip of approximately five and a half hours.

The crew area in the Canberra was very cramped when compared with the Valiant, and would have been more than a little uncomfortable for five and a half hours, the 9 Squadron ORB commented that 'the main features of the sorties were the cold and the length of them'. In his account, Fred Jones referred to the discomfort when wearing the flying helmet for long periods:

> It was always a relief to remove the Bone Dome [slang for the protective outer helmet] together with the helmet and liner that contained the earphones. One's ears got very sore after an hour or so with the helmet in place and there is no way to relieve that feeling upstairs unless you take off the helmet – not an easy job when airborne.[46]

Ground crew working on an RF-84F of the ER.4/33 Squadron of the French air force after its return from a reconnaissance sortie. One of the crewmen can be seen opening the large cover for the camera bay to recover the film: all the post-strike photographs used in this book were taken by RF-84Fs. (Albert Grandolini Collection)

What did cause some concern for Canberra crews operating from Malta was the fuel state on the return legs of these long sorties; 139 Squadron ORB again:

> One very [unreadable] feature was the unfamiliarly low readings in the fuel gauges; for most of us it was the first time we had operated the Canberra anywhere near its limits in range.

As with the details on other raids, there are some anomalies in the records, this time relating to the number of aircraft and squadrons taking part from Malta. The ATFC report[47] is specific that there were four Marker Canberras and six bombing Canberras from Cyprus, with four Valiants and eight Canberra bombers from Malta; a total of 14 bombing Canberras. Cull[48] has the same numbers – probably taken from this source. However, in the signal sent from the C-in-C in Cyprus to the Chiefs of Staff on the morning of 1 November, detailing the raids launched during the night of 31 October/1 November, the numbers were 'eleven Canberras and four Valiants'. The number of Canberras is completely wrong. In addition, to add to the confusion, the 101 Squadron ORB[49] details a Canberra flown by Flying Officer Bull as taking part in a raid on Abu Suweir, 'with No. 9 Squadron'; the 9 Squadron ORB has no mention of this, nor does Cull. Bull's sortie would increase the number of Malta Canberras from eight to nine, which does not agree with any of the other sources.

INCHAS AIRFIELD

The bombing campaign opened with the recalled raid on Cairo West, during the evening hours of 31 October. The last attack of this opening phase was in the early, pre-dawn hours of 1 November; the target was the airfield at Inchas, just a couple of miles north of Cairo International. Three squadrons from Cyprus took part in the raid: Squadron Leader Kearns led the two markers from 139 Squadron, with the rest of the stream made up of eight Canberra bombers from 27 Squadron and seven from 61 Squadron. However, not all from 61 Squadron got airborne. Flying Officer Kenyon in WH915 was leading Flying Officer Price in WH918 as they began to taxi out for take-off. At this point Kenyon appears to have selected his undercarriage 'up', which collapsed the nose-wheel on the tarmac. Price, following close behind, had no room to go around 915, and so was unable to take part in the raid. Kenyon was subsequently court martialled and given a year's imprisonment for failing to carry out the mission. According to Kyle,[50] Kenyon's defence was that he disagreed with the Suez operation but had pressed the wrong button by accident. His is the only recorded case of active dissention with Operation Musketeer. Although only five crews from 61 Squadron took off to take part, the flying log in the squadron ORB still shows Price (who was prevented from going by Kenyon's action) as having got airborne at 02:55, landing back at 03:30, but with the note that Duty [was] Not Carried Out (DNCO).[51] At the same time, the flying log has no mention of Kenyon's deliberate abort. The only reference to this incident is in the summary of the events for November: "On the morning of 1st [sic] Nov., the nose-wheel of WH915 collapsed when the aircraft was started up."[52]

Today we would say that Kenyon had been 'airbrushed' out of the squadron record. WH915 was sent up for an air test on 9 November, presumably to check the repairs on the nose-wheel.

Leaving Kenyon and Price on the taxiway, the rest of the bomber stream headed for Inchas with the bombers each carrying 6 x 1,000lb bombs and the two marker crews having 2 x 1,000lb Target Indicators and 3 x 1,000lb bombs; a total of 84 bombs were dropped on the target. There were no hang ups and Kearns (M1 for the raid) described the briefing as 'adequate' but with 'insufficient time for accurate flight planning and target study'. Additionally, he stated that there should have been more information on enemy gun positions to allow crews to better plan their attack dives and bomber crews needed to be 'more aware of the need for bombing accuracy, especially on pinpoint targets'.[53] The post-raid report expanded on this point.

> The raid was carried out in the early morning and no difficulty was experienced in target or aiming point identification. [...] Midway through the raid, the bombers were directed by Marker Leader to bomb the secondary marker as the Primary marker was no longer visible. The T.I.s were released from 1400 feet and burst at 800 feet. The target was marked on time but the bombing was not as consistent as would achieve a high concentration of bombs round the aiming point. In fact, only a small number dropped within normally acceptable limits of error. Despite this, the object was achieved and two of the three runways were out.

The 27 Squadron ORB put more of a gloss on their bombing effort; 'Bombing was accurate and the Master Bomber reported the effective cutting of the runway intersection'. By 0530, the crews were back on the ground, no doubt ready for a quick debrief and some breakfast.

9

CREWS: DOWNTIME ON BASE BETWEEN RAIDS

Operations continued for a few more days, as we will see, but it is worth mentioning one or two comments from Fred Jones' account to give a little insight into their time out of the cockpit. The RAF bases at Nicosia and Luqa were overloaded with aircraft and crews during Musketeer, and the Officers' Mess would not have been able to accommodate all of them. Jones and his colleagues were in tents on Nicosia, as they discovered after their transit trip out from the UK:

> We were tired following our early departure from UK and found our bell tents, which were to be shared by four people and hence were very cramped with all our kit and camp beds. Dust was everywhere and it was quite warm but thankfully dry.[1]

During the following night, having returned from the raid on Almaza, they experienced their first air raid warning. Like many of us who have heard the fire warnings in hotels, they did not take it too seriously:

> There was one scare in the early morning as we attempted to sleep and that was the wail of the air raid warning siren making us all get out of bed. Our shelter was supposed to be the Officers' Mess building but we just stuck our heads out of the tent and waited. [...] Out of the blue there came a whistling sound which sounded just like the familiar sound of a bomb falling and then after a silent pause came the loud clatter of a

This photograph shows Mather's crew in what was probably a posed press or publicity photo. Flight Lieutenant Roy Mather is on the left, his co-pilot Flying Officer Ross and the three rear crew, (though not necessarily in this order) Flying Officer Cole, Flight Lieutenant Bruton and Pilot Officer Stratford. The person on the right is probably the technician, the Crew Chief. The Crew Chief would normally only fly with the crew if they were dispersing away from their home base. He would not have flown on the operational sorties. (Courtesy Rob Mather, via John Dillon)

The crew of a Valiant bomber debriefing on their return from a bombing sortie. (Albert Grandolini Collection)

> stone rattling on the tin roof from a nearby hut. A pregnant pause and then the typical service cheer 'hoorah' sounded out around the area and we returned to our beds.

Later that day the crews discovered the cause of the night's alarm, Jones again:

> It had occurred as a result of an unidentified blip coming down from the north on the radar warning systems and was suspected to have been a Russian reconnaissance aircraft. It was believed to have circled overhead and then returned from whence it came.

In places, Jones' account reads a little like that from aircrew on standby in the Second World War:

> There was another buzz going round that we were on another 'Op' that night, with a briefing around 16:30 [this would be Cairo West]. We trundled back to our tents and lay on top of our beds trying to relax as much as possible. In for lunch again and this time a salad with lots of tinned pilchards, one of my favourites.

Although the crews met little opposition on their raids, from EAF fighters or ground-based anti-aircraft fire, there was always the chance of being hit:

> On the 3 November, around 0830, we were called to a briefing and the old routine went into action. Butterflies in the tummy, the nervous nip to the toilet, yet everything seemed to be going well.

Anyone who has read memoirs written by Second World War aircrew, or seen old documentary film from that time, will be familiar with crew and squadron mascots, and the idea of 'lucky' aircraft. Fred suggests that the jet age was no different. Even though his aircraft, WD993, had an unserviceable fuel pump, they still felt comfortable with the same airframe:

This photo appears to show a crew collecting their gear after a post-raid debrief. (Albert Grandolini Collection)

> It is strange how often sentiment and luck go together when under such circumstances. I gave up being superstitious a long time ago because if you allowed such a thing to affect one's pattern of life, particularly when flying, then life can become tricky and confused. When flying you do not want to spend time thinking something could go wrong because you had either not done something or you were not carrying a lucky token. It is not a good idea to be worried but the question must be asked though, "Why does it feel better flying the same aircraft?"

Once the crews had landed from their operations, had

A Valiant crew having a well-earned mug of tea following a raid debrief. (Albert Grandolini Collection)

been debriefed and had a meal, there was a period of wondering 'what next', as Jones recalled; 'It was rather difficult to retire to one's bed and relax not knowing when or where things would happen. At least the early evening had now passed and that meant no night sortie'.

10

1 NOVEMBER: EVENING RAIDS

The first night of the RAF's bombing campaign had gone reasonably well, albeit with one raid recalled and the bombing accuracy on the others being variable at best. During the target planning meeting held on the morning of 1 November, Cairo West was chosen as the first to be attacked, to make up for the aborted raid of the previous night. This would be followed by the airfields at Luxor, Fayid and Kasfareet. The transmitters at Cairo Radio were selected during the evening meeting for a daylight raid on the morning of 2 November.

As with the aborted raid, Cairo West was to be attacked by a combined force of Valiants and Canberras from Malta and Cyprus. Four crews from 139 Squadron on Malta would act as markers, with seven Canberras also coming from Nicosia; two from 10 Squadron, two from 15 Squadron (although the summary of the month's activity in the ORB claimed that three crews took part), and one bomber crew from 139 Squadron. Malta contributed six Valiants from 138 Squadron, four Canberras from 12 Squadron and three more from 109 Squadron. Between them, they dropped 147 bombs.

One of those taking part was Fred Jones and his crew and he wrote later that it was dusk when they came out of the briefing tent, and dark by the time they had strapped in. As they started engines 'The airfield and taxi lights, plus all the aircraft navigation lights, were all that was visible'. As the aircraft moved out in order into the stream 'there was no radio chat between the aircraft and the Tower' but occasionally 'the surface wind and speed direction was passed out in the clear as a test broadcast'.[1] As Jones' turn came round, he increased power and after rotate and with the undercarriage up, he settled into the climb and the crew assumed the normal en-route checks as they headed for the target. At the top of climb, the navigation lights were turned off and the cockpit lights dimmed.

Once again, Flight Lieutenant Slater was M1 for the raid with M2 and the two Flare aircraft also coming from 139 Squadron. They took off with standard loads for the marking and flare tasks and had no hang ups. The weather was good, with a clear sky and no haze; it was also moonless. On this occasion, Slater reported that they had had sufficient planning time, and the briefing was adequate. With a clear night, they had 'easily identifiable pinpoints on the Western side of the Delta'. As well as the visual fixes, they were also able to navigate using the Nicosia beacon and Blue Shadow.[2] At least one of the Valiants was carrying a green proximity TI, which was dropped approximately 200 yards outside the airfield perimeter on a south-westerly bearing. Slater states that he and M2, 'released flares on a timed run, ignoring the green T.I.'.[3] The flares dropped by Slater, from 8,000 feet, did not ignite in the air, but three of them did when they hit the ground; luckily M2's flares all operated correctly and the target 'could be clearly seen beneath them'. Before the bomber stream commenced their run-in, M1 dropped his TI on the centre of the runway intersection, while M2 dropped his on the runway threshold. According to Slater's report, the timing of the Marker and Flare crews was 'excellent, as was the accuracy of the marking. M1 dropped his TI from 1,200 feet, M2 from 1,400 feet and he judged that the TIs were within 20 yards of the aiming point.

Slater and his three cohorts were followed in by the Valiants and Canberras on their bombing runs. John Foot, in a Valiant recalled that the Navigator Plotter 'was on his belly, doing the business lying in the nose using the T4 bombsight, dropping the bombs visually, while I backed him up with the NBS and following the target on the H2S radar screen'.[4] Foot stated that their 12 bombs were dropped with 'impact fusing' while Jones' bombs from his Canberra had delayed action fuses and dropped from 25,000 feet. Valiants and Canberras, dropping iron bombs visually from heights up to 40,000, are hardly likely to be accurate on a pinpoint target, such as a runway intersection. When Slater reported that '85% of bombs fell within target area' he was probably referring to the whole airfield as the target. According to his report, the main runway was hit by a stick of five bombs, cratering it on one side; another runway received a direct hit in the centre and other bombs fell 'amongst buildings and installations'. Although he reported the crews' response to instructions from the markers as 'very good', 'two sticks badly undershot the aiming point by at least 2,000 yards' – a little over a mile. Once again, the post-raid report recommended that there should be wind-finding crews flying at the same height as the main bomber force to increase bombing accuracy. Egyptian opposition to the raid was again minimal. Jones stated that they had to expect defensive fire from the 'radar controlled Russian-type guns which so far nobody had witnessed' however, Slater reported that there appeared to be '4 light A.A. and 4 heavy A.A. guns firing at commencement of raid. Firing ceased abruptly when bombs started falling. Firing was wild and inaccurate'.

With the attack complete, Jones turned north, climbed to 30,000 feet and began the 'long monotonous flight back' and after flying the trombone pattern, started his approach to Nicosia:

> Then we can see the lights of the runway well ahead of us, the flare path, clearance to land comes up to the R/T and we squeak a landing and run the full length of the 9,000 feet of runway to clear at the end and taxi back to dispersal.[5]

No doubt Jones' crew, like the others, was glad to have a quick debrief, a meal and then back to their tents for a good sleep.

LUXOR

While Jones and the other crews were returning from their sortie, others were on their way to bomb Luxor airfield. Once again, the times recorded in ORBs and the ATFC reports differ, but the TOT appears to have been around 8-9 p.m. on 1 November. For this raid, all aircraft were based in Cyprus: four Marker crews from 139 Squadron, eight bombers from 27 Squadron, six from 10 Squadron, five from 15 Squadron and a lone crew from 61 Squadron. As a further example of the unreliability of the times recorded in the different sources, the 139 ORB flight log indicates that one crew was airborne at 1820, two at 1825, and the fourth (on the same raid) at 1625. The airfield at Luxor is situated on the east bank of the Nile, some 275 nautical miles south of Cairo, making the raids on this target the longest mounted from Cyprus.

The raid was led by Squadron Leader Kearns of 139 Squadron; he was M1 and the 'Squadron Boss', Squadron Leader Mallorie, followed him as M2. Incidentally, Kearns' post-raid report mistakenly dates the attack as 2 November.[6] The night was starlit, with fine weather and while there had been an 'adequate' briefing Kearns felt that, again, there had been insufficient time for the marker and main force to complete detailed target study – as the bombing results were to prove. On this run, probably because of the closeness of track to the Nile, there was 'adequate scope' for the use of Blue Shadow, the radio compass, Eureka and pinpoint visual navigation. All 20 of the bombing Canberras carried 6 x 1,000lb bombs but one crew from 27 Squadron were unable to drop two of them 'due to a premature release of its tail fins prior to take off'.[7] Given the clear night and the relative ease of locating the target, the bombing should have gone better than it did. Kearns' report gives some reasons for the poor results:

> From 8,000 feet on the initial flare run Marker 1 was able to pinpoint his position but not to release his flares visually and the initial drop was about 1 mile North East of the target. In the light of these flares, Marker 1 identified the target and directed subsequent flares to be released over the aiming point. [...] The bombing all undershot the aiming point a distance up to 2 miles in some cases, and no notice was taken by the main force crews of marker leader's instructions to overshoot the aiming point; consequently the raid was a failure and information at present

Ground crews moving trolleys with 1,000lb bombs around Canberra B.Mk 6s of Nos. 12 (WH960) and 9 Squadron (WH954) at RAF Hal Far during the Suez Campaign. (Richard Caruana Collection)

Ground crews seen while preparing an unidentified Canberra B.Mk 6 for a mission, during temporary deployment to the Mediterranean area in October 1956. (Albert Grandolini Collection)

Two Canberras from No. 10 Squadron, seen waiting to be loaded with 1,000lb bombs – like the six that can be seen on the trolley towed by the tractor in front. Six bombers from this squadron hit Luxor airfield late on 1 November 1956. This squadron's aircraft were the only bombers of the RAF to wear camouflage colours during the Suez Campaign (for details, see Colour Section). (Albert Grandolini Collection)

A row of Canberra B.Mk 6s from No. 101 Squadron (first five aircraft), and No. 9 Squadron (five aircraft in the rear). Both units were involved in nocturnal air strikes on Kasfareet on 1 November 1956. (Albert Grandolini Collection)

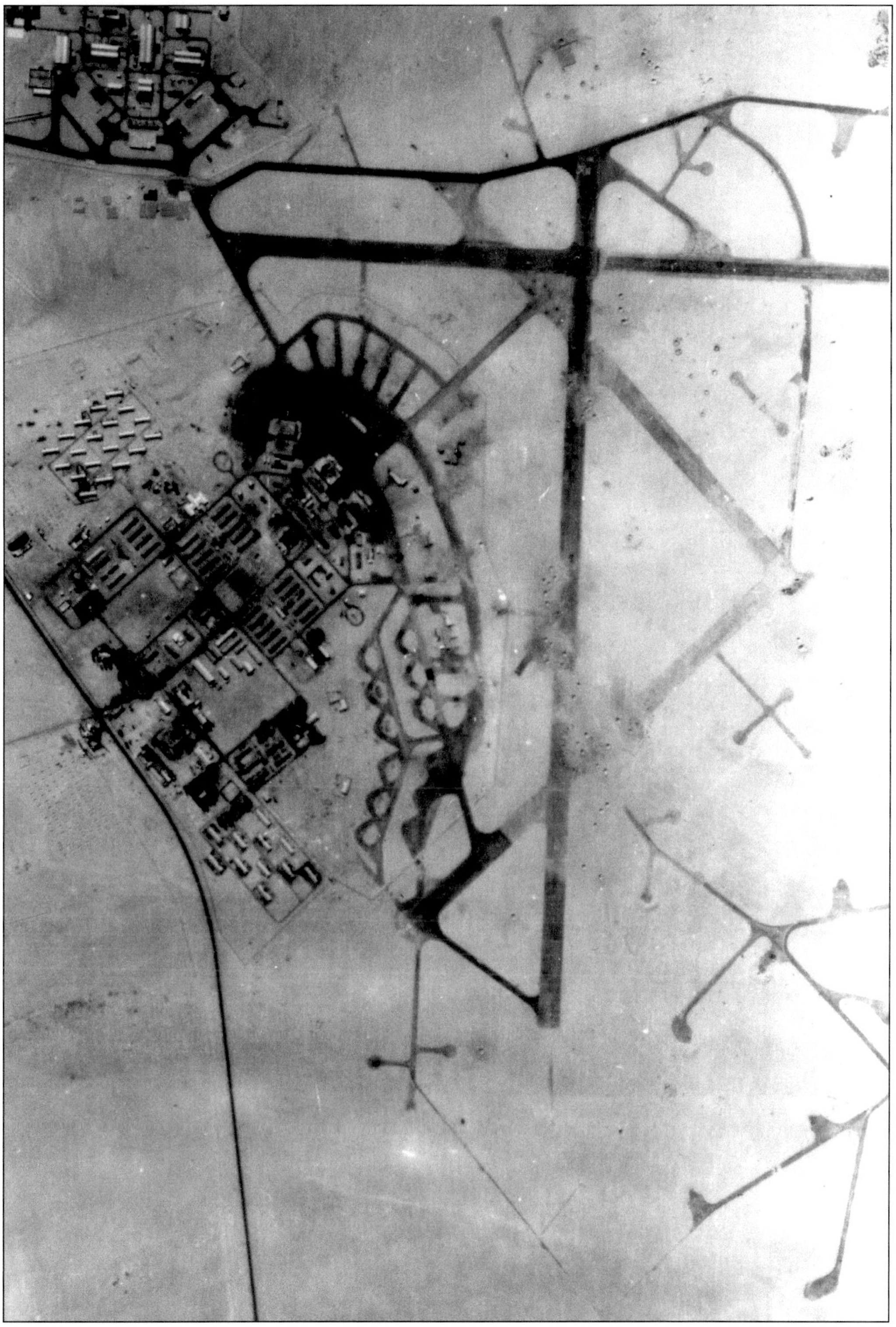

A section of a reconnaissance photograph of Fayid AB taken by an RF-84F from an altitude of 30,000ft. Notable are dozens of craters well positioned down the main runway and at least close to its intersections with multiple older runways (meanwhile used as taxiways). (Albert Grandolini Collection)

available indicates that none of the 24 Il-28s on the airfield were damaged nor were the runways out.[8]

The bombers, who released their 118 bombs (there would have been 120 but for the problem on the 27 Squadron aircraft) from heights between 25,000 and 29,000 feet, were a little more optimistic in their assessment of the effort. The 15 Squadron ORB declared that the targets were well marked 'and bombing appeared to be highly successful'.[9] Recognising the poor quality of the bombing Kearns made some recommendations, but the short duration of Musketeer meant that it would not be possible for them to be fully implemented: a bombing wind should be passed every five minutes before H-hour – he does not suggest by whom, but presumably a 'wind finding' crew; 'Main Force crews must study the approach to the target more thoroughly so where possible the approach and aiming point can be checked visually'. Those who planned the raids must also bear some responsibility for the results as crews consistently complained about inadequate time for pre-flight briefings. His final suggestion was fairly radical; he suggested that the marker crews should also have a 'ground attack capability' to make the raid more effective. Presumably, this was based on the fact that the Marker and Flare crews came in at a much lower altitude than the Main Force.

FAYID

As well as the raids that night on Cairo West and Luxor, attacks were also mounted against the airfields at Fayid and Kasfareet, both of which are fairly close to Kabrit. The latter airbase is on a promontory between the Great Bitter Lake and the entry to the last few miles of the Canal, just north of the town of Suez. Kasfareet is only about a mile due east of Kabrit, on the bank of the Bitter Lake, while Fayid lies just a few miles north-west of Kasfareet, again on the West Bank of the Great Bitter Lake. Both should have been relatively easy to identify by the features of the lake. For the attack on Fayid, crews were allocated from Malta and Cyprus. Marking for the main force were four Canberras from 18 Squadron (Cyprus), with three Canberras from 44 Squadron and three from 61 Squadron delivering the bombs. Four Valiants from 148 Squadron led the Malta bomber stream with the CO, Wing Commander Burnett, dropping the primary proximity marker. The aiming point for the bombers was the intersection of the NS/EW runways. Burnett's crew assessed their marker as having been a 'direct hit on the aiming point at 1930 hours'.[10] Their marker was followed by their 11 x 1,000lb bombs, at 1945, and the ORB has the interesting comment that these were 'also' dropped using the NBS, which implies that both proximity marker and bombs were

This photograph of Flying Officer Fred Jones was kindly supplied by his son, Howard. Fred flew with 44 Squadron on Musketeer and his account of the operations is featured in this book. Although Fred flew with 44 the photo shows him standing alongside a 139 Squadron aircraft, and he has their squadron crest on his flying suit. (Howard Jones Collection, via John Dillon)

not dropped visually. They estimated that these fell 100 yards from the aiming point, on a bearing of 270 degrees. The second Valiant crew was Squadron Leader Ware's and they dropped their TI at 1931, with their 11 bombs released at 1946, which they estimated as impacting '200 yards from the target'. If these were correct, then it was very good bombing by both crews, given the technology of the time. Crew three estimated their 12 bombs (no TIs for them) as hitting 500 yards from the target on a bearing of 350 degrees and crew four claimed their 12 as 200 yards, also on a bearing of 350. According to Keightley's ATFC report, 'the runways were heavily attacked'. Although we do not know the track made good of the bombers during release, it is difficult to see how sticks of 12 bombs, with the given impact points (presumably of the first bombs to hit), could have done much damage to the north-south and east-west runways. The example of the Vulcan bombing Port Stanley on the Falklands demonstrates how difficult it is to hit a runway; only one of the 21 bombs in their stick doing so.

The raid on Fayid was relatively uneventful, except for two incidents, both of which involved 109 Squadron. Flight Lieutenant Pembridge and crew did not take-off because during the pre-flight checks they had a 'sticking tailplane actuator'.[11] On the Canberra, the whole tailplane moved to vary the angle of incidence and control the pitch of the aircraft. A faulty actuator could cause the tailplane to move to the limits of its travel, irrespective of commands from the pilot; the loss of some aircraft and crews has been attributed to this problem. The other crew to have their day spoilt was that of Flying Officer Hawkins, although they bombed successfully, they had an engine failure on their return to Malta but executed a single-engine let-down and landing. Interestingly, while WJ783 (Pembridge's aircraft) had an air test for the actuator problem on 3 November, there is no mention in the ORB of WJ982 (Hawkins' engine failure) having an air test before flying again on an operational sortie on 4 November. Presumably, the engineers gave it a ground run and passed it as serviceable.

KASFAREET

The last of the attacks on the night of 1 November was on the airfield at Kasfareet, towards the southern end of the Great Bitter Lake. For this raid, four Canberras from 18 Squadron on Cyprus marked the target for the bomber force flying from Malta, four Valiants (two from 207 and two from 214 Squadrons) and eight Canberras (four from 101 and four from 9 Squadrons). As with the earlier raids, there was very little opposition from anti-aircraft guns or fighters. The Valiants all had a full load of 12 x 1,000lb bombs, while the eight Canberras in the bomber role each had four bombs. According to 9 Squadron ORB, the crews did a cruise climb to the RV then maintained their height for the bombing run. Their bombs all had a 0.14 second delay; the other squadrons make no note of this detail. All crews returned safely to Luqa, except F/O Hilliard who had to divert to El Adem in Libya because of his low fuel state. The squadron ORB[12] records that he was only on the ground for a little over two hours to allow him to refuel and continue back to Luqa, arriving a little before 5 in the morning.

11

'PHASE 1...HAS BEEN ACHIEVED'

In Chapter 3, the three phases of Musketeer Revise were outlined, of which Phase 1 was the 'Neutralisation of the Egyptian Air Force'. By the end of D+1 (1 November), and with the raids detailed above all complete, the C-in-C believed that the EAF had been so reduced as to be of very little threat. This view was reinforced by the almost total lack of effective Egyptian defence against the raids of the RAF bombers. Air Marshal Barnett, the Air Task Force Commander, expressed his satisfaction with the progress in Phase 1 in glowing terms:

> The destruction of the Egyptian Air Force as a fighting entity was achieved in less than 36 hours by a composite allied force of bombers, land-based and carrier-borne ground attack aircraft that had never operated together before and came under the control of the Air Task Force Commander only two and a half days before the operation started.[1]

Only later in his report did Barnett mention that the bombing of Abu Suweir, Luxor and Kasfareet 'was disappointing' and that aircraft could still operate from those runways. However, the military action by Britain and France was now coming in for international condemnation, with the USA – furious with the action of the Europeans – drafting a UN resolution for an immediate ceasefire (at the same time Soviet tanks were moving into Hungary). The need to keep civilian casualties to a minimum meant that the psychological warfare element of Phase 2 could not be carried out and 'only military targets were to be attacked'[2] during this phase. The only exception to this directive was that 'an attack [was] to be launched on the Cairo Radio Station'. At 1835Z on 1 November, the Air Task Force HQ signalled the bomber wings that while it was 'too early to judge the extent of success [of the bombing] it appears likely that phase two of Operation Musketeer can start sometime tomorrow D plus 2'.[3] Accordingly, Phase 2 started at 0800Z on 2 November. From this point on, the attacks on airfields were intended to 'contain' the EAF following its neutralisation.

ATTACK ON CAIRO RADIO, 2 NOVEMBER

The only non-military target allowed in Phase 2 was Cairo Radio, or to be more exact, the transmitters at Abu Zabal, Cairo. The initial planning for Musketeer had included a daylight raid on these buildings, 'concurrently with the first strikes by the ground attack forces'. The fact that it did not take place at that time was attributed by the ATFC to 'political restrictions'.[4] The decision to mount the raid was made during the evening targeting conference, 1 November; the transmitters would be attacked at 0850Z on the following morning. This was to be the first daylight raid by the bombers and would be carried out at low level; in the context of Musketeer that meant 3,000 feet, rather than the 100-300 feet that would be expected today. The height of 3,000 feet was chosen to allow for the possibility of the bombs exploding on impact,[5] rather than after a short delay. If that happened at 300 feet, then the explosion would be likely to cause serious damage to the attacking aircraft.

Although all previous sorties by the bombers had experienced very little opposition from the EAF, this raid would be escorted by twelve F84F fighters from the French air force.

All the bombers came from squadrons based on Cyprus. The Air HQ was not prepared to risk the Valiants in daylight operations and the low level phase, and subsequent climb to height for the return leg, would have put the fuel consumption beyond the limits of the Canberras at Luqa. The bombers from Nicosia were led by two markers from 18 Squadron with the following 18 Canberras coming from 10 Squadron (three), 15 Squadron (three), 27 Squadron (four), 44 Squadron (four) and 61 Squadron (four). The 18 bombers all carried 6 x 1,000lb bombs. This should have meant that 108 bombs were dropped on the target, yet the ATFC report states there were 98 and a signal from the Air Task Force HQ in the early hours of 3 November claimed that '19 Canberras from Cyprus aimed 104 x 1,000lb bombs at Cairo Radio station in early daylight'.[6] Conscious of the need to limit any civilian casualties, a warning was given that an attack was imminent as the message from AFHQ to the Ministry of Defence on 5 November made clear, 'It can be stated with certainty that anti-casualty precautions have never before been given such attention or prominence in a military campaign of this kind'.[7]

In the event, the bombing was much less successful than the crews or the commanders had hoped; the ATFC report skipped briefly over the results; 'Most bombs undershot or overshot. One hit reported very close to target'.[8] With 20 Canberras involved, and 108 (or 104, or 98) bombs dropped, this was a poor result, although the station did stop transmitting for a few days. A number of reasons were put forward for the mediocre bombing. The T4 bombsight was intended for visual bombing from high altitude in which case, with a forward throw of the bomb of some miles, the sighting angle on the T4 would be quite small whereas, at 3,000 feet, it would be of the order of 70^0, and so very difficult to sight properly.[9] The Canberra crews had had little training or experience at low level, as the 44 Squadron ORB noted in the comments on this raid:

> Low level attacks were found to be the most difficult due to the high speed (330 knots) used, coupled with a high degree of turbulence. Also some difficulty in navigation was encountered due to the lack of experience of crews in map reading at low level approximately 3,000 feet over the desert.[10]

When Musketeer was complete, the Under Secretary of Defence involved himself in a written discussion with the various Air Staff Chiefs regarding the visual bombing training undertaken by Canberra crews prior to Suez; this is one of the comments by the VCAS on the need to attack at 3,000 feet:

> It was, therefore, an extremely difficult pin-point target for Canberra light bombers and was made more difficult by the clouds of dust from the first few bombs dropped. *If it could have been arranged, it would have been a better target for ground attack aircraft.* [author' italics.]

With no opposition, all aircraft returned safely to Cyprus.

Canberra B.Mk 6 from No. 109 Squadron seen in the process of taking-off from RAF Hal Far, during the Suez War. (Albert Grandolini Collection)

For those raids that came after Cairo Radio, some changes were made to the bombing technique. As this attack had encountered no opposition, 'it was evident that a condition of complete air superiority had been attained'[11] and consequently the second raid on Luxor airfield (planned for that night) would now take place 'just before dark'. In addition, because the remaining targets 'called for more precise bombing', the bombers from Nicosia were to operate by day and at a lower altitude, 'about 8/10,000 ft.' Those based on Malta would continue to fly night attacks 'as it was undesirable to hazard the Valiants by day'.

LUXOR, 2 NOVEMBER

By Friday 2 November, the crews who had flown out from the UK to Malta and Cyprus were becoming accustomed to their new routine; briefing, flying, eating, sleeping and then briefing again. Some, like Fred Jones, had left home with only a light overnight bag:

> We had only travelled to Cyprus with a minimum of personal kit, no KD [Khaki Dress for the summer], just battle dress plus a civvy shirt and a pair of slacks. The battle dress was already getting quite 'high' because I had flown in it beneath my flying overalls.[12]

At the morning target conference, 2 November, Luxor airfield was chosen for a second attack, with a TOT of 1515Z; it was considered safe to allocate a time shortly before last light as the previous attacks, especially the morning's raid on Cairo Radio, had met little opposition. According to the comment in the 15 Squadron ORB, one of the aims of the raid was to 'attempt to destroy the Il-28 aircraft remaining on the airfield after the first raid [during the previous night]'.[13] Once again, Luxor was to be a target just for the Cyprus-based squadrons, led by Squadron Leader Mallorie and his four markers from 139 Squadron. The 139 crews carried a mixed load; M1 and M2 both had two target indicators and 3 x 1,000lb bombs, while M3 and M4 actually flew as bombers with 6 x 1,000lb each. Unfortunately, two of the four had hang ups, M1 had one bomb that did not release and M4 had three of them. The report does not mention whether or not they returned to base with them or managed to jettison over the sea.

A French reconnaissance photograph of Luxor airfield, seen after being raided by Canberras of the RAF. Notable is smoke rising from the wreckage of at least two Il-28s that were knocked out. (Albert Grandolini Collection)

As well as the nearby airfield no longer in use, the Egyptian Army's storage depots at Huckstep received lots of attention from the RAF bombers. This low altitude reconnaissance photograph shows extensive damage to multiple hangars, and rows of heavy military vehicles. (Albert Grandolini Collection)

As well as the four markers, there were 18 Canberra bombers from a mix of squadrons; 10 Squadron (three), 15 Squadron (five), 27 Squadron (three), 44 Squadron (three) and four from 61 Squadron. Although it was felt safe to mount a daylight raid, the bombers were escorted for part of the route by French fighters.[14]

The briefing for the raid was considered 'adequate' by Mallorie as Luxor had been attacked previously and the same route was to be used on this trip. However, he did state that the target material was 'out of date', but he does not say in what way. Navigation to the target was made easier because of the daylight, making map reading easier. The route was 'via a distinctive island on the Red Sea coast, a bend in the Nile north of Luxor and thence direct to the target',[15] the identification of which 'was straightforward in the light of the sunset'. The timing for the attack was judged to have been good although the main force (the 18 bombers) were about two minutes late. Mallorie's description of the marking plan is worth giving in full:

The marking plan was for Marker 1 & 2 to mark each end of the largest concentration of Badgers on the airfield and for them to be followed by Markers 3 & 4 dropping sticks of bombs, aimed diagonally at each runway, from 10,000 feet. The aim was to give the defences something to think about during the marking, and if possible to damage the runways. The T.I's [sic] were dropped at each end of the East-West taxiway and the East-West runway was damaged. Unfortunately, the attack on the North-South runway was frustrated by Marker 4's three hangups. Otherwise, the plan was fairly successful though unnecessary in the face of the one gun defence system, but it must have created some confusion if only by having four attacks from different directions and different altitudes within a very few minutes. [16]

Having marked the target, Mallorie stayed in the area as Master Bomber and included his assessment of the bombing effort in his report:

> By the time bombing started the target was in darkness and the T.I's [sic] showed up well. Bombing was accurate and was directed from one T.I. to the other and then to a mid-point. Five healthy fires were left at the end of the attack. The bombing accuracy was such that the attack could profitably have been switched to the North-South perimeter track where other Badgers were dispersed. [N.B. Mallorie is the only source referring to Badgers and may well have meant Beagles – the Il-28]

In spite of Mallorie's comments, later bomb damage assessment showed that, like many of the Suez raids, Second World War techniques and old iron bombs did not allow for pinpoint bombing. The ATFC report judged that raid to have been 'not very successful' and the photos from a later PR sortie indicated that Luxor was 'still serviceable and there were still about 20 serviceable Beagles there which constituted a threat to our airfields in Cyprus'.[17] The raid had not been incident free. Just after take-off, Flying Officer Haywood (27 Squadron) was unable to retract the undercarriage and was forced to land after jettisoning his bombs over the sea. Another 27 crew, Flying Officer Miller's, was unlucky enough to sustain light damage over the target, as reported in the ORB; 'Light intermittent flak resulted in [his] aircraft receiving slight damage in the tailplane'.[18] The squadron report also makes the interesting comment that 'V.T. fused bombs were used for the first time in this attack', there is no similar comment in the other squadron reports. Given that VT fused bombs tended to be airburst, a little above ground, it does seem as though these were intended to destroy the aircraft on the ground with shrapnel and air burst, rather than runway penetration. On this note, Mallorie also commented that parked aircraft are better targeted by ground attack aircraft, rather than bombers.

HUCKSTEP, 2 NOVEMBER

At the target conference on the morning of 2 November, Huckstep Camp (to the east of Cairo) was chosen as the target for two raids that evening, the Time on Target was to be 1930Z and 2030Z. Huckstep was primarily an army camp with barracks, ammunition stores and vehicle parks and the attacking force for both attacks would again be a mix of aircraft from the bomber wings at Malta and Cyprus. At this point, the communication problems that have been mentioned in previous sections manifested themselves. The orders for the two raids were signalled 'in clear' to Malta at 0915Z and 0920Z but they were received in a corrupt form and corrections were called for:

> These were passed but a complete breakdown in communications between Cyprus and Malta occurred. When communications were resumed, a message was received from Malta requesting a postponement since the desired Time on Target of 1700Z could not be achieved.[19]

The delay in resuming communications meant that the aircraft could not be prepared in time for the required sorties. The attacks were deferred to 1930Z and 2030Z respectively. However, by now the met forecast for the time of the take-offs and landings had become available and Bomber Wing Malta cancelled their participation in the second attack owing to predicted adverse landing conditions. These changes, and the way in which the various documents were written up after the event, have led to some confusion over the Huckstep raids on 2 November. In his post-raid account, Squadron Leader Kearns (M1 from 139 Squadron) gives the date of the raid as 3 November instead of 2 November. The 139 Squadron ORB flying log, as well as the other participating squadrons, all give the date as 2 November. Kearns may have written his report on 3 November, causing him to incorrectly date the attack. In his book, Cull states that 18 Squadron supplied four crews for the first raid with Kearns and eight crews (four markers and four bombers) for that at 2030Z. He correctly notes that the Malta contingent for the second attack was stood down due to weather, but goes on to say that the 'eight Canberras of 18 Squadron from Cyprus [went on] to strike again at Huckstep'.[20] The ATFC report for 2 November has only the 1930Z attack listed with the four Canberra markers, five Valiants (two of the seven launched had problems and did not drop) and 15

Another reconnaissance photograph shows massive destruction of entire rows of M4 Sherman tanks of the Egyptian Army, stored at Huckstep. (Albert Grandolini Collection)

A photograph of the Valiant B.Mk 1 serial WP201 taken after the war. (Albert Grandolini Collection)

Canberra bombers. The eight crews from 18 Squadron that Cull shows as taking part in the second Huckstep raid did not go. The only crews from that squadron to fly against Huckstep on 2 November, according to the squadron flying log, were the four that followed Kearns on raid one.

The Valiants from Malta were led off by the Squadron Commander, Wing Commander Oakley. Unfortunately, the wheels on his aircraft failed to retract after take-off and the crew had to jettison their bombs over the sea, burn off fuel to get down to landing weight, and land back after an hour and a half. The raid continued with the bombers from Malta and Cyprus joining up for the attack on the Target Indicators laid down by the Marker Canberras. The eight Canberras from Nicosia bombed from 25/26,000 feet, dropping 48 x 1,000lb bombs. The record does not state the height from which the Luqa bombers made their release but the Valiants were probably at about 40,000 feet. Not only were Oakley's crew unable to deliver their 12 bombs but Squadron Leader Collins found that the bomb doors on his aircraft were not able to open on the bomb run, and he had to return to Luqa with a full bomb load. Flying back in this configuration increased the Valiant's fuel consumption, 'leaving him very little fuel on arrival at Luqa'; with his low fuel state, he was probably given a priority approach, as Collins' was the first Valiant crew to land.[21] In his account of the raid, John Foot (Navigator Radar on Flying Officer Catlin's crew, 138 Squadron) stated that, after landing 'there was great consternation' among the ground crew; 'we had a hang-up on one of the carriers', so they had landed without being aware that they still had a bomb on board.[22]

The issue of bomb fusing, and the difference between penetration and airbursts, has already been touched on and is relevant in the case of this raid on Huckstep barracks and camp. As it was an attack on barracks and vehicle parks, rather than runways and airfield infrastructure, VT fuses were employed to deliver airbursts, as Ford describes in his account:

> [T]here was a lot of tented accommodation with the Egyptians under canvas. Therefore, to make life really uncomfortable for the enemy, and to get the maximum effect, it was decided to drop the stick of 1,000 pounders with airburst fusing set to go off at 1,000ft.[23]

At the targeting conference on the evening of 2 November, it was decided to launch three daylight raids the following morning, two of them against the barracks and stores at Almaza, close to Cairo International, and one raid against the railway marshalling yards at Nfisha (variously spelled as Nefisha and Nifisha in different sources), close to Ismailia and a little west of the Canal where it enters the Great Bitter Lake.

The two attacks on Almaza were timed to hit only 20 minutes apart, with TOT of 0800Z and 0820Z. Given the closeness in time of the two raids, it is reasonable to discuss them as one, as the ATFC report does in its summary. Both were led by markers from 139 Squadron, and followed by Canberras from other squadrons at Nicosia; M1 for the first attack was Flight Lieutenant Slater with Flight Lieutenant McNeil in the same role for the second. All four markers carried two red TIs and 3 x 1,000lb bombs. It must be said from the outset that the combined effort against this target was less than successful. The following comments are largely drawn from the post-raid reports of Slater and McNeil.[24]

While the briefing for the two raids was considered 'adequate', there was insufficient time between the end of the briefing and take-off. Worryingly, McNeil stated that the section of the brief that dealt with the target was inadequate – 'target maps were not available' – which he considered a 'pity […] as Almaza airfield provided a very good feature for identifying the target'. It should be remembered that the target for these raids was not the airfield per se, but the barracks. The route out to the target was flown at low level by the markers on both raids and as it was daylight, visual map reading was the main navigation aid. Slater names some of the places en-route and the coasting-in point at Ras el Bar is easily identified, followed by Damietta. On arrival in the target area, the marking did not go well. Slater, on the first raid, was 'unable to release stores due to a mechanical failure'. M2 on that run (Flying Officer Elton) was 'unable to release stores on shallow dive, but released on a bombing run at 8,000 feet. T.I's [sic] did not appear to ignite'. The target had to be identified visually by the bombers as 'no markers seen'. McNeil, on the second raid, had to confirm the target 'both by the results of the previous raid and also by the close proximity of Almaza airfield'. Unfortunately the markers' problems on this raid did not stop there; 'Due to some inexplicable miscalculation of fuel consumption, both marker 1 & 2 arrived in the target area short of fuel'. As a result, they had to leave the area before their bombing run, were unable to assess the results of their raid's bombing, and had to return with their bombs. Slater reported that the bombing on the first raid 'did not appear to be accurate', with a considerable number of the bombs falling on the airfield, rather than the barracks. Although both marker leaders reported opposition as light, it would appear that Slater (unbeknown to him) had received slight damage from ground fire; a 0.303 bullet had caused damage to the main spar and a fuel tank,[25] but he and his crew returned safely. As well as the embarrassment of returning after a fuel miscalculation, McNeil had a bird strike on the way home; 'Flying at low level Marker 1 hit a bird which damaged the starter cowling of the starboard engine'. The ATFC report put rather more of a gloss on the raid than Slater and McNeil's reports would seem to warrant:

> Two marker and 20 other Canberras released a total of 123 x 1,000lb bombs from 25-29,000 feet. Reports indicate that *85% of bombs fell in the target area*; many fires were seen.[26] [author's italics.]

The damage to Slater's aircraft (WT371) had later, unfortunate consequences. A 9 Squadron crew (Flying Officer Collins, pilot) had ferried a replacement aircraft to Nicosia and were detailed to fly 371 back to the UK. Shortly after take-off they lost power in one engine and on overshooting for a second approach, Collins 'put power on the one remaining good engine, causing the aircraft to flip over and crash short of the runway',[27] all on board were killed.

12
RAIDS OF 3 NOVEMBER

NFISHA RAIL YARDS

The daylight raids of Saturday, 3 November, continued with the attack on the large railway marshalling yards at Nfisha. As with other raids, some of the reports differ slightly in the number of crews participating, and from which squadrons. The ATFC report states that Marker Canberras were followed by 20 bombing Canberras, with 126 bombs delivered. This account differs from Cull's in the designation of the squadron providing the markers. Cull[1] has two crews from 139 Squadron but their flying log[2] only records crews flying against Almaza barracks that day. However, 18 Squadron's[3] specifically states that they provided two marker crews for operations against 'Ismailia', the yards at Nfisha. They also had three crews in the 'main force' on that raid. Senior commanders sometimes like to experience operations at the 'sharp end' and Air Marshal Barnett (Air Task Force Commander) was no exception. In order 'to assess the situation more accurately',[4] he flew with Group Captain Woodroffe's crew on this raid to Nfisha. The success of the raid was on a par with the others flown against Egypt, there was 'extensive damage with locos and rolling stock destroyed',[5] but reports from the crews only estimated 50 percent of the bombs as falling 'in the target area'.[6] The six aircraft on the raid carried 36 x 1,000lb bombs between them, of which 'several direct hits were observed and recorded by camera'.[7] The ATFC report suggested that the crews had probably had difficulty identifying the aiming point as this was 'quickly obscured by fire and smoke from burning oil tankers'[8] among the rolling stock.

A low altitude reconnaissance photograph, showing numerous craters and significant damage to the Nfisha Railyard and three trains. (Albert Grandolini Collection)

Port said, seen while under air attack on 4 November 1956. (Albert Grandolini Collection)

This led to the introduction of revised marking procedures for some of the subsequent attacks.

WEATHER POSTPONEMENT

The morning raids on Almaza and Nfisha should have been followed by further attacks during the evening of 3 November and the morning of the following day, but circumstances dictated otherwise. During the targeting conference held on the morning of 3 November, the island of El Agami and a concentration of tanks at Huckstep were both selected as targets for the Malta Bomber Wing, with TOT of 2230Z and 2330Z, respectively. However, as the day progressed, heavy rain at Malta made full load take-offs hazardous and with an unfavourable forecast for the expected landing times, which would prejudice the recovery of aircraft the decision was taken to cancel both raids. The following morning's conference, 4 November, rescheduled them for 1645Z (El Agami) and 1745Z (Huckstep) that evening. However, the weather was not the only reason for the bombing pause. The O.C. Bomber Wing at Nicosia revealed that the armament personnel, especially those responsible for fusing the bombs, 'were showing

Another view of Port Said and the local port facilities. (Albert Grandolini Collection)

signs of strain' because of the workload and it was decided to stand down his bomber aircraft for 24 hours.[9] As a result of the weather on Malta and the need to rest the armourers on Nicosia, there was a pause in the bombing between the morning raid on Nfisha on 3 November and the night raids on El Agami and Huckstep on 4 November. The postponement of the raid on 3 November afforded one Valiant captain the opportunity to participate in a little local sport, as the 214 Squadron ORB records; 'Sqn. Ldr. [sic] Petrie took part in a game of Polo with the Marza club at Luqa'.[10]

EL AGAMI

The Anglo-French assault on Egypt had been strongly criticised from the start by the United Nations, especially America:

> By D+3 it was becoming increasingly obvious that it would be difficult to justify in world opinion the maintenance of an air offensive, whether on military or civil targets, until the assault forces were available to land on D+6. [...] As a result, orders were issued by the Allied Commander-in-Chief to the

Valiant B.Mk 1 serial WP215 – operated by No. 138 Squadron during the Suez Campaign – seen later during its career. (Courtesy Roy Mather, via John Dillon)

Armourers pushing a trolley with three 1,000lb bombs under the fin of a Canberra B.Mk 2 at RAF Nicosia. (Albert Grandolini Collection)

Task Force Commanders to launch an airborne assault on the morning of D+5.[11]

With the truncation of the schedule for Musketeer, and the bringing forward of the airborne assaults, the targets selected from 4 November were more about preparing for the landings than attacking the EAF – in the view of the air commanders this had now been neutralised. El Agarni (there are different spellings in the sources) was not considered to be ideal for the bombers because of the dispersion of the radar and coastal guns that were the real targets; they were more suited to ground attack than high-level visual bombing. However, the Joint Planning Staff desired this part of the coast to be attacked 'in the hope that enemy attention would be directed from the intended point of assault (Port Said)'.[12] The raid was considered 'unsuccessful' for a number of reasons; the following are taken from the ATFC report, squadron ORBs and Greethurst's account in *FlyPast*. The marking did not go well with some of the Target Indicators bouncing from land into the sea, where they were extinguished, five of the Canberras did not drop their bombs as 'no T.I's [sic] were seen', (they were dropping from 30,000 feet). Two of the Valiants also saw no TIs, one dropped using NBS, but their bombs undershot by 2 miles, the other suffered unserviceable NBS, so did not drop. According to the 109 Squadron ORB the poor bombing was a result of the target not being correctly marked by the Pathfinder force (18 Squadron) as they had encountered heavy light anti-aircraft fire. Greethurst wrote that his crew did a timed run and while he could 'clearly see the lights of the target below us' they bombed 'blind' from about 40,000 feet. The crews were not helped by the route and target information passed from Headquarters: 'Owing to an error in transmission [...] the position of the I.P. was incorrectly received at Malta. This led to the attack being carried out on a Northerly heading instead of North Easterly, as planned, and made the approach to the target more difficult'. All in all, it is difficult to take too many positives away from this raid, it was unlikely that many of the radars or guns on the ground were hit, but it may have succeeded in its aim to divert Egyptian attention away from Port Said.

HUCKSTEP

With the airborne assaults now brought forward to 5 November, the army base at Huckstep was the target for raids on the night of 4 November with two more during the morning of the following day. The first of these attacks was marked by four Canberras from 139 Squadron, with a mixed bomber force of Valiants and Canberras from Malta. Marker 1 for the raid was Flight Lieutenant North and he reported that he and M2 dropped their flares from 8,000 feet, 'where two very accurate red proximity T.I's [sic] had been dropped by Valiants, practically on the top of each other'.[13] Although North judged the timings to have been 'excellent', the flares gave 'adequate illumination' and the marking was 'comparatively easy', he estimated that only 40 percent of the bombs fell on the briefed target, although 75 percent fell in the camp area. The 109 Squadron ORB reported that 'Nearly all the bombs of the raiding force undershot the target quite badly'.[14] Reg Ellicott was a navigator on 214 Squadron on this raid and put his recollection in an email:

> On my Suez op we carried 12 x 1000lb HE bombs and after pressing the button to release them I counted them falling – 1, 2, 3, 4 and then no more, 8 having hung up due to the electrical connection failing to the upper tier [of the bomb carrier].[15]

The Canberras, as was standard when flying from Luqa, only carried four bombs and the 101 Squadron ORB makes the interesting point that the fusing was obviously intended for different effects; one of the four was VT fused for detonation

50 feet above ground, two had instantaneous fusing with the remaining bomb set for penetration and a delay of 0.14 seconds.[16] We have noted on an earlier raid that a crew had to divert to El Adem because of a fuel shortage and on this raid Flying Officer Hart (101 Squadron) had to make a similar diversion, this time because of a low oxygen state.

13

RAIDS OF 5 NOVEMBER

HUCKSTEP

Monday, 5 November (D+5), was the rescheduled date for the joint Anglo-French airborne assault of the Canal Zone. In support of these drops, the bomber wing at Nicosia flew bombing missions against tank concentrations at Huckstep Camp, as well as marking the Drop Zones (DZ) for the paratroops. The day was also significant politically as the Secretary General of the UN had set midnight New York time, 7 a.m. in Cairo, as the time by which hostilities should cease in order to comply with the resolutions of the General Assembly.[1] Needless to say, this did not stop the day's sorties. The two raids on Huckstep were separated by two hours with TOTs of 0630Z and 0830Z, and both were mounted by squadrons in Cyprus.

The first was led by Flight Lieutenant Slater (139 Squadron), both marker crews carrying 4 x 1,000lb Target Indicators, behind them in the bomber stream were 14 Canberra bombers; two from 139, and six each from 44 and 61 squadrons. Following the Nfisha raid (as noted above) it was considered necessary to change the bombing technique to improve the accuracy of subsequent attacks, consequently offset marking (see Chapter 5) was employed on these two raids. Slater, as M1 for the raid, was briefed to mark the aiming point as being 500 yards short of the target centre on the run-in heading of the main force.[2] In his report, Slater stated that he released his TIs at a height of 1,200 feet, with no line error but a 50 yard overshoot. He was presumably satisfied with the marking as M2 held onto his TIs until the main force had completed his bombing, he then ran in and dropped his on the centre of the target hoping to start some fires. The bombing was considered to have been the 'most concentrated yet', with 80 percent falling within the target area and the bombers responding well to Slater's instructions as Bomber Leader. In his report Slater wrote that on completion of the bombing by the main force, he made a run over the target 'and could see craters fairly close to tank concentration, the nearest one being about 25 yards, but no craters among the tanks'. On earlier raids the crews had recommended that the bomber force should be accompanied by a 'wind finding' crew, flying at bombing height, to pass an accurate wind to the bombers to improve accuracy; this was the first time that the technique was implemented on Musketeer. Flight Lieutenant McNeile's crew, 139 Squadron, took on the role and drew the following comment in Slater's report; 'a better concentration of bombs was observed, thus justifying their use'. As the campaign was almost over there was little chance to develop the role.

The second raid on Huckstep, two hours later, was led by two marker crews from 18 Squadron, Flight Lieutenant Bennett as M1, followed by 19 Canberra bombers, one from 61 Squadron and six each from 10, 15 and 27 Squadrons. This attack was similarly 'successful', though not by today's guided-munitions standards. Two of the TI's fell 500 yards east of the aiming point, as planned for an offset attack, but they were obscured by smoke and the two from M2 impacted east-south-east of the first two. The two marker crews did not observe any direct hits on the aiming point, although one stick fell 'within 100 yards of the tanks'. M1 estimated that the main weight of the bombs fell within 800 yards of the target while the bombing crews gave a more optimistic estimate of '200 to 400 yards North West of the aiming point'.[3]

At this point in Operation Musketeer, with only days left in the American Presidential election race, Russian tanks and troops moving into Hungary and international opinion very much against the Anglo-French invasion, the involvement of the RAF bomber wings was almost complete. At the same time as the first wave of Canberras was hitting Huckstep, crews from 18 and 139 Squadrons were marking the Drop Zones for the airborne assaults.

By 5 November 1956, extensive damage to the infrastructure along the Suez Canal was clearly visible. This was the famous Firdan Railway Bridge, dropped by the Egyptians to prevent the use of both it and the the crucial waterway. (Albert Grandolini Collection)

MARKING OF DZS

On 5 November, the RAF bombing campaign came to an

A four-engine Hastings used for transporting personnel, paratroopers and cargo. (Albert Grandolini Collection)

A view of the engines of a Shackleton maritime patrol aircraft, behind which a company of paratroopers is lining up to board a transfer from Malta to Cyprus. (Albert Grandolini Collection)

end, but for Eden to meet his objective of humbling Nasser and controlling the Canal it would be necessary to have boots on the ground; troops would be delivered by air and by sea. As the title of this book makes clear, this account does not detail the ground operations, which have been well covered by other historians.[4] However, the marker squadrons at Nicosia had an important role to play in the delivery of these troops and their supplies; they would mark the DZ for the different airborne drops, including the French.

The French and British parachutists were to go in on 5 November, with the seaborne landings taking place on the following day. Because the whole operation had been truncated,

Operation Omelette (the original plan for the airborne assault) was now known as Telescope, as outlined in the Air Task Force Commander's subsequent report:[5]

> Operation "Telescope", which was written *some 48 hours before it was adopted*, was an *ad hoc arrangement* to land the parachute forces a day in advance of the main assault. The purpose behind this plan was to get a force ashore ahead of a possible order for a cease fire by the United Nations. [author's italics.]

As Barnett's last sentence makes clear, the timing of the military operation was being driven by the need to manage world opinion. In preparation for the airborne assault, the three Task Force Commanders sailed on HMS *Tyne* from Limassol at 1300Z on 4 November, to a point 30 miles off the Egyptian coast. A little before 6.30 in the morning, local time, two marker crews from 18 Squadron and two from 139 took off to mark the Drop Zones. Squadron Leader Chamberlain (18 Squadron) was M1 for the flight to Gamil airfield on the Egyptian coast, a little west of Port Said; H-hour was 0515Z. Squadron Leader Kearns (139 Squadron) was M1 for the French DZ at El Raswa (with the same H-hour), a mile or two south-east of Gamil. The marking was straightforward, except for M2 on the El Raswa sortie having two of his TIs hang up. This did not really matter as the targets were easily identified and the crews considered eight TIs to be excessive. The third sortie to mark a DZ was led by Squadron Leader Mallorie (139 Squadron), with an H-hour of 1315Z. This was for Hastings transport aircraft to drop heavy supply loads at Gamil airfield. Again, the marking was straightforward and while they also considered that eight TIs were not necessary, Mallorie made the comment that their smoke 'gave a useful indication of the wind speed and direction',[6] which would have been useful for the navigators on the Hastings aircraft to determine the correct point for dropping their parachute loads. In his account of Musketeer, Fred Jones described the take-off and recovery of the transport aircraft:

> They had been taxiing around the perimeter track and moving into position one after the other and then taking off at about 3 minute intervals. The whole process seemed to take a long time before the last one disappeared down the runway and climbed slowly away into the dawn that was just beginning to appear. [...] It was not until mid-morning when the first of the Hastings came back to the airfield and soon there was a stream of them landing and taxiing back to their starting points.[7]

14
6 NOVEMBER: CEASEFIRE

The bombing of Huckstep Camp on the afternoon of 5 November, drew a line under the contribution of the Malta and Cyprus bomber wings to Operation Musketeer. By D+6 (6 November) instructions were received from the Allied Commander-in-Chief 'that all further bombing was to cease'[1] and all operations planned or under consideration for that night and 7 November, were to be cancelled. With the overcrowding at Nicosia and Luqa, this could lead to a large number of aircraft on the ground being vulnerable to an attack 'from a re-vitalised Egyptian Air Force',[2] and the decision was taken to send some of them home to the UK; three Valiant squadrons from Malta and three Canberra squadrons from Nicosia were to return 'forthwith'. Some squadrons and crews were kept in theatre for a number of weeks in case the war started up again, 27 Squadron did not go home until 22 December. In true RAF style, the cease-fire was an occasion for a celebration, as the 27 Squadron ORB for 10 November, tells us:

> Preparations were made for a squadron party to be held in one of the H.Q. tents. The party was a great success and provided a welcome opportunity for all to "let off steam".[3]

One of the Valiant co-pilots wrote that during the bombing they had expected 'publicity and applause' for their involvement and were surprised to learn of 'discord and argument at home'.[4] Goodall and his colleagues may not have been so surprised had they been aware of the political shenanigans taking place in Whitehall. At a Cabinet meeting on the evening of 4 November, the PM stated that as the Israeli representative at the UN had accepted a cease-fire proposed under an Afro-Asian resolution, and the Egyptians had previously agreed to a cease-fire, there was a heavy onus on the British and French governments to also accept the cessation or they would be responsible for 'the continuance of hostilities which it had been the professed intention of their intervention to stop'.[5] As the airborne and amphibious troops had not yet been inserted into the Canal Zone, this was not the state of affairs that Eden wanted. By the end of their meeting, they heard that the Israelis had now rejected the cease-fire terms, and the landings would take place. With events moving ahead in the UN to try to bring an end to the hostilities, and Russia (which had moved into Hungary) also threatening to get involved, different proposals were put forward in New York. At the same time, Eden's government was trying to find a way to 'regain the initiative in bringing hostilities to an end',[6] while carrying with them the more moderate sections of world opinion. Having taken Britain to war, Eden needed to show the people at home that British forces had achieved the aims of the military intervention, as he stated in the meeting:

> [I]f we accepted a cease-fire at a moment when we had only just occupied Port Said and had not yet secured Ismailia and Suez, we should appear to have fallen short of that effective occupation of the Canal area which we had publicly declared to be one of our objectives.

Britain would accept the cease-fire, provided that the international force that the UN proposed to send in to the Canal Zone was competent to secure the objectives set by the

UN. However, the Anglo-French force 'would cease fire *at some point during the day*, the exact time to be determined in the light of operational circumstances'[author's italics]; presumably this would be when Eden had achieved his aim.

The political endgame is not the subject of this account (Kyle and Tunzelmann's books cover this), but a few comments from the minutes of the Cabinet meeting held at 11.15 am, 8 November, give a flavour of Eden's predicament. The government had to be ready for the possibility of the Egyptians restarting the conflict:

> Reconnaissance indicated that the airfields in the neighbourhood of the Canal were being rapidly repaired; and it was possible that, under cover of the cease-fire, the Egyptian losses of aircraft were being made good from the Soviet Union.[7]

With the cease-fire in place, troops on the ground in the Canal Zone and many of the bombers on their way home, 'the troops at Port Said and in Cyprus were exposed to a risk which the Commander of the Anglo-French forces was unwilling to accept unless the United Nations could guarantee them against Egyptian attack'. The British were in a 'pickle' with world opinion against them and having infuriated Eisenhower's administration; the position was summarised in the Cabinet minutes:

> We had been compelled to bring military operations to a halt before our objectives had been fully attained. We were now faced with a situation in which the Suez Canal was blocked; our oil supplies from the Middle East were at risk; alternative supplies from the Western Hemisphere could not be counted upon, especially in the absence of financial aid from the United States.[8]

Alternatively, as one writer put it: 'The only sound was that of the air being let out of British and French imperial pretentions'.[9] When Eden gave the go ahead for Musketeer, following the dinner at 10 Downing Street on 26 July, this was probably not the position he had expected to be in.

CREWS GO HOME

With the bombing phase complete, and the continuing space constraints on Malta and Cyprus, it was necessary for some of the crews to return home to the UK. On 6 November, at 6.00 p.m. in the UK, a signal was sent to the headquarters in the Middle East; aircraft were to start returning 'at once', with ground crews following as soon as transport was available. However, equipment was to be retained in theatre to allow operations to be resumed if necessary and once the crews were back on their home bases they had to be held 'at four hours readiness to take off and return to present bases'. It was emphasised that those squadrons held ready to return 'must be those already 'Musketeer' experienced'.[10] This was followed by a signal stating that on 7 November, or as soon as practicable thereafter, three Canberra squadrons and ground personnel were to leave Cyprus while three Valiant squadrons were to return from Malta.[11] 10 Squadron flew home to Honington on the night of 7/8 November, taking about nine hours (including two hours at Luqa) but crews then had a rota of two days at four hour standby with a relaxation to 12 hours every three days. Fred Jones (44 Squadron) gave an account of the trip home that would have been typical for all the Canberra crews returning from Cyprus and having to stage through Luqa:

> On the evening of 6 November, we were told to get our kit packed in readiness for an imminent move early the following morning. [...] Hungary was still in the headlines. [It was dark when they went to briefing the following morning.] We took off in the dark and headed West which meant that we would continue to fly in darkness all the way to Malta. We climbed to a higher altitude and soon the frost settled and formed around the inside of the canopy on the bare metal.[12]

As Jones' account demonstrates, the leg from Cyprus to Malta highlighted the limited navigation aids that were available to the Canberra crews who had been bombing Egypt:

> We seemed to be flying an awfully long time before eventually changing course northwards towards Malta. There was a Eureka beacon (navigation system) at Luqa airfield and we had expected to pick it up very soon after the north turn but, alas, heard nothing. We continued to fly north for an interminably long time. [...] Normally what should have been a two and a half hour trip was stretching towards three hours. [...] It appears that the winds had been vastly different from that given at the Met briefing. There had been a strong jet stream that had affected us all and meant that we had all been miles south of the required track and the northward turn had actually taken place over the coast of North Africa!

The rest of the trip was uneventful and they arrived over 'the green hills of Suffolk' around midday on 7 November. One of the squadrons that had to spend time at Cyprus, following the cease-fire, was 27. These crews were unable to begin returning until after 17 December, when they were delayed by the Lincolnshire fog:

> Unfortunately the weather at Waddington precluded a landing there on Wednesday afternoon [19 December] and the night had to be spent in a diversion at Valley. The following day fog still persisted at Waddington and a landing at Binbrook followed by a coach journey for the last 20 miles had to be made.[13]

On their arrival home, many crews found themselves on standby to return, and this must have been galling and disruptive to private lives after being away on operations. The Air Ministry, in a signal on 7 November, issued the details of operational aircraft in the UK that they expected to be available to return if needed:

- One Valiant and one Canberra PR7 at three hours for possible use by V.I.Ps. Remaining Canberra PR7s at 24 hours.
- Two Canberra B6 [marker aircraft] at three hours and remainder at 24 hours.
- Valiants withdrawn from Malta. 15 at four hours. Remainder released for training but must be able to redeploy as quickly as possible.
- Canberra B2s withdrawn from Cyprus. All at four hours.[14]

The bomber crews, Valiants and Canberras, had done what had been asked of them with the tools available. As with a football team, they could only play the team opposing them, accepting the ground and the weather as common to both sides. It must be said that the RAF was lucky to be up against a relatively inept opponent, whose anti-aircraft defences were not effective enough to overly concern the bomber crews and where the weather was good on all but one day, so helping to mitigate their lack of navigation aids.

15
COMMENTARY AND ASSESSMENTS

Lessons, political and military, can always be drawn from operations like Musketeer but as we have seen in previous chapters, the plans of the commanders were subject to a certain amount of political interference, particularly the bringing forward of D-3 and the consequential impact on photographic reconnaissance sorties. The February 1957 report on Musketeer notes in its conclusion that:

> It would be dangerous to draw military conclusions from Operation 'MUSKETEER' because it was coloured and confined by political considerations from start to finish.[1]

Air Marshal Barnett made a similar comment relating to the planning process:

> The joint planning at Task Force level, which lasted for over two and a half months, proceeded smoothly in spite of being continually affected by political considerations.[2]

The military commanders for the Suez operation were not unique in finding that their plans were subject to political exigencies, although it is reasonable for them to point out where this 'interference' affected the intended military results. In Barnett's report he drew attention to the attack on Cairo Radio, which the RAF were made to postpone until 2 November and which was 'only semi-successful and clearly required a repeat attack', but 'the trend of events' precluded this. In Barnett's opinion, 'had the attack been delivered in its planned position in the programme there would unquestionably have been time for a decisive re-attack'. Right up and till the paratroop invasion on 5 November, the commanders were having their plans reviewed; Eden and his ministers were concerned about possible civilian casualties, the Americans, the UN resolutions and the Russian moves into Hungary. On 4 November, Anthony Head (Minister of Defence) and General Sir Gerald Templar (CIGS) flew into Nicosia in Canberras to reassess the war plan: "Everything was to be reined in so that the operation looked as much as possible like the peacekeeping initiative Eden was trying to pretend it was."[3]

Against this background, how well did the bombers operate and how effective was their contribution to Operation Musketeer?

WAS THE BOMBING EFFECTIVE?

In the 10 years following the end of the Second World War, the world had changed: the nuclear bomb had been dropped over Japan and Europe had entered the Cold War. The RAF had moved on from the age of the Lancaster to that of the jet bomber, the Canberra and the Valiant – with the Victor and the Vulcan to make up the family of 'V' bombers. These aircraft were intended to fly independently (gone were the large bomber raids of the Second World War), at high level, to drop their nuclear weapon on large targets – cities and industrial complexes. Against such targets, pinpoint accuracy was not required given the devastation a nuclear weapon was known to cause from the attacks on Japan. In this role the GEE-H, Blue Shadow, Green Satin and visual bomb sights, together with the NBS that was being rolled out for the V-bombers, were adequate navigation and bombing aids. However, at night over Egypt, with poor target information due to the lack of PR (a result of the political interference), and a lack of navigation aids, the crews were frequently relying on visual map reading – luckily, the good weather allowed this. These limitations were compounded by briefings that were frequently criticised by the marker crews as being inadequate and lacking in target detail. Barnett's report stated that 'the bombing accuracy was seriously impaired by the inadequate navigation and bombing facilities available'; the size of some of the bombing errors have been pointed out in previous chapters.

The RAF had to mount the bombing component of Musketeer from two bases in the Mediterranean, Luqa in Malta and Nicosia in Cyprus. The 91 Canberras and 24 Valiants could not all operate out of Cyprus (alongside the squadrons already based there) although that would have been ideal as it was so much closer to the Egyptian targets than Malta. Basing the Valiants at Luqa provided no real operational problems but it was different for the 29 Canberra crews who had to fly from there. The return trip from Malta to Cairo, with fuel reserves for the slow trombone recovery pattern (covered previously), meant that these Canberras were operating at the limits of their range, and instances have been noted of crews having to divert because of their low fuel state on their return legs. This range limitation meant that these crews could only carry four bombs on a sortie, instead of the six that the Cyprus crews could drop.

The bombing technique was reminiscent of that employed in the Second World War, in spite of the fact that the Valiant and Canberra aircraft were 'state of the art' – the V-bombers took on the role of Britain's nuclear deterrent and the Canberra design was bought and modified by the USA, where it had entered service in 1953 as the B-57. Target marking was developed by 139 Squadron only months before the start of Musketeer; the comment by their commanding officer (Squadron Leader Mallorie, as he then was)

Portrait-photo of Flight Lieutenant Roy Mather, DFC, AFC, a Valiant pilot during the Suez Campaign and – indirectly – an important source for this book. (Courtesy Rob Mather, via John Dillon)

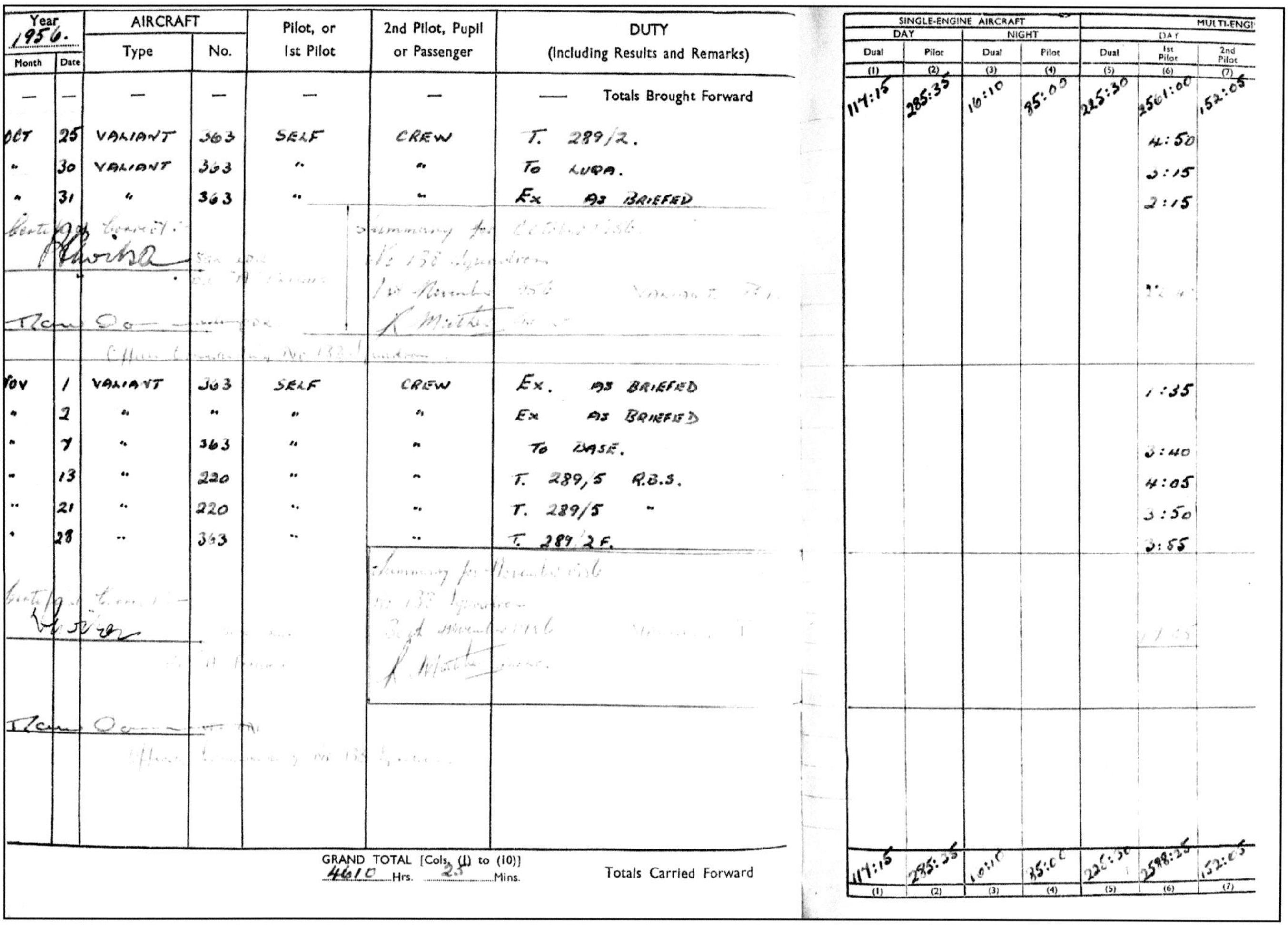

Year 1956 Month	Date	AIRCRAFT Type	No.	Pilot, or 1st Pilot	2nd Pilot, Pupil or Passenger	DUTY (Including Results and Remarks)	Multi-Engine Day 1st Pilot (6)
—	—	—	—	—	—	Totals Brought Forward	2561:00
OCT	25	VALIANT	363	SELF	CREW	T. 289/2.	4:50
"	30	VALIANT	363	"	"	To LUQA.	3:15
"	31	"	363	"	"	Ex AS BRIEFED	2:15
NOV	1	VALIANT	363	SELF	CREW	Ex. AS BRIEFED	1:35
"	2	"	"	"	"	Ex AS BRIEFED	
"	7	"	363	"	"	To BASE.	3:40
"	13	"	220	"	"	T. 289/5 R.B.S.	4:05
"	21	"	220	"	"	T. 289/5 "	3:50
"	28	"	363	"	"	T. 289/2 F.	3:55

GRAND TOTAL [Cols. (1) to (10)] 4610 Hrs. 25 Mins. Totals Carried Forward

A scan from Roy Mather's pilot logbook, listing his sorites flown in Valiants on 25, 30 and 31 October, and 1, 2, 7, 13, 21 and 28 November 1956. All operational sorties were annotated 'Ex. as briefed'.(Courtesy Rob Mather, via John Dillon)

to the RAF Historical Society in 2008 is revealing of the way they were left to get on with it:

> At the time I was, and in retrospect I remain, astonished at the rather casual way we were left to develop the marking system which was suitable for Canberra aircraft but without any high-level guidance which I can recall, apart from clearance to drop armaments.[1]

Mallorie's problems went beyond the 'casual' way in which his squadron was left to develop the marking technique, as a couple of comments in his November 1956 report make clear. To bring his unit up to the required strength of 12 aircraft and 14 crews, four aircraft and four crews were attached to 139 from 109 Squadron:

> These attachments were only completed shortly before operations began with the result that crews whose capabilities were not fully known by the Squadron Commander had to be sent on vital sorties.[5]

Additionally, because they were to operate outside of their normal role, training was not what it should have been:

> All crews had dropped practice bombs and T.Is [sic] by night, seven pilots and navigators had limited experience of dropping flares and four pilots had very limited experience of dropping T.Is [sic] in flare light. No crew had been constituted with an observer for longer than 12 weeks and the observers had almost negligible night map reading training.

In his conclusions, one can sense that Mallorie did not consider the bombing techniques employed during Musketeer as being the right ones for the modern age: "If target marking is to be used in the future against more determined opposition the technique will need revisions."[6]

The initial aim of the bombing campaign had been the neutralisation of the EAF and this objective was achieved within the first couple of days. However, this had not been because of pinpoint bombing; the ATFC report stated bluntly that the target marking and bombing 'were not up to the expected standard',[7] and 139 Squadron's conclusion on the marking technique they had developed and used was that it was 'only usable when the defences are light'. Airfields in Egypt, the main targets for the bombers, were large areas of sandy ground with only about 10 percent taken up by runways and hard standings; the post-raid reports indicate that the majority of the bombs that fell on the airfields did not hit the runways. A more determined opponent would have been able to continue flying and make life much more difficult for the bomber crews.

During Operation Musketeer, the bomber wings dropped 1,884 bombs in 18 raids on 13 targets: 'This number of bombs would have been considered adequate for only one relatively small target during the latter period of the 1939-45 war'.[8] This comment in the Air Task Force Headquarters' report on the bomber participation

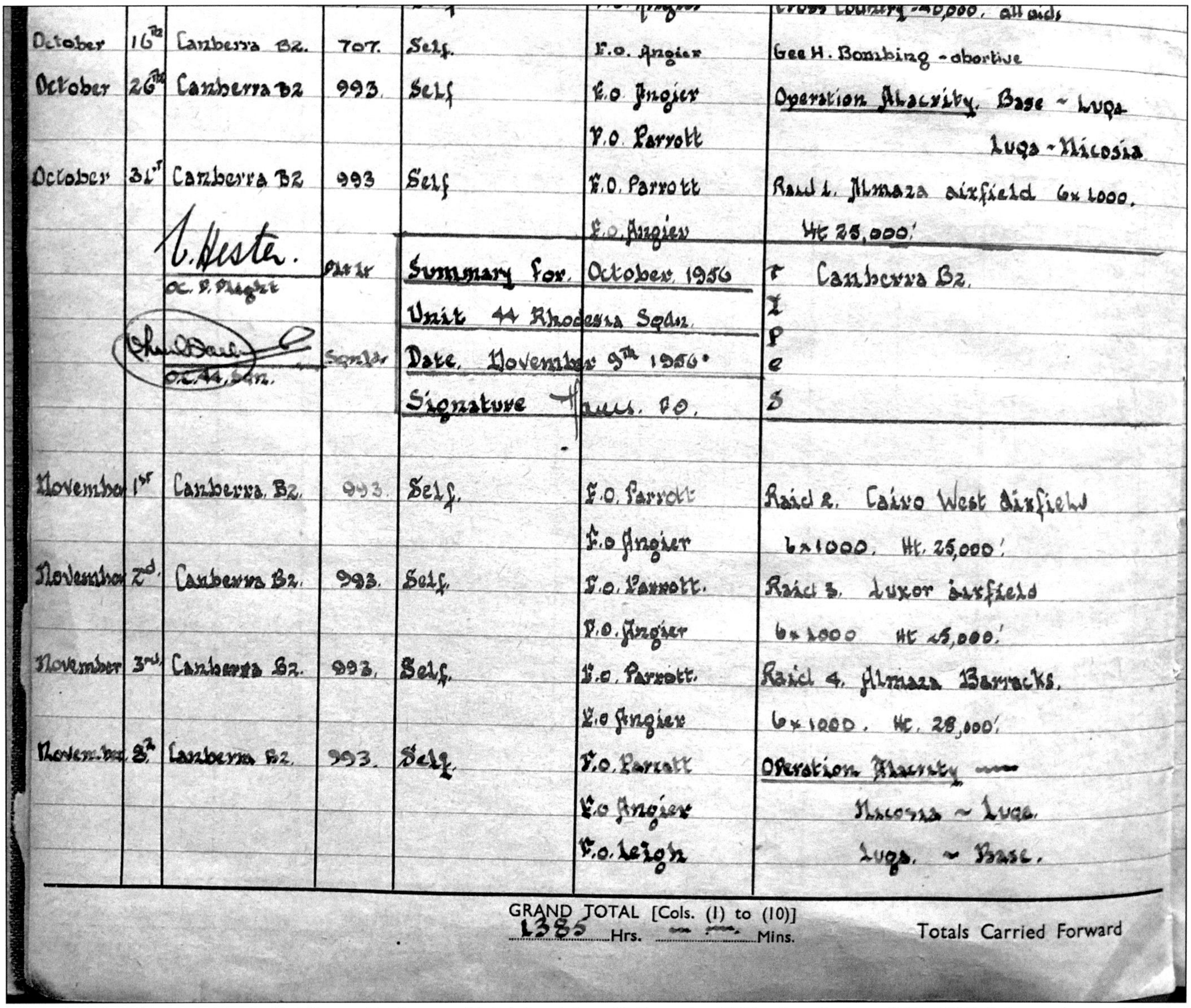

October	16th	Canberra B2.	707.	Self.	F.O. Angier	Gee H. Bombing - abortive
October	26th	Canberra B2	993.	Self	F.O. Angier F.O. Parrott	Operation Alacrity. Base - Luqa Luqa - Nicosia
October	31st	Canberra B2	993	Self	F.O. Parrott F.O. Angier	Raid 1. Almaza airfield 6x1000. Ht 25,000'
				Summary for	October 1956	Canberra B2.
				Unit 44 Rhodesia Sqdn.		
				Date November 9th 1956.		
				Signature		
November	1st	Canberra B2.	993.	Self.	F.O. Parrott F.O. Angier	Raid 2. Cairo West airfield 6x1000. Ht. 25,000'
November	2nd	Canberra B2.	993.	Self.	F.O. Parrott. F.O. Angier	Raid 3. Luxor airfield 6x1000 Ht 25,000'
November	3rd	Canberra B2.	993.	Self.	F.O. Parrott. F.O. Angier	Raid 4. Almaza Barracks. 6x1000. Ht. 28,000'
November	8th	Canberra B2.	993.	Self.	F.O. Parrott F.O. Angier F.O. Leigh	Operation Alacrity — Nicosia - Luqa. Luqa. - Base.

GRAND TOTAL [Cols. (1) to (10)] 1385 Hrs. — Mins. Totals Carried Forward

A scan from Fred Jones' pilot logbook, listing sorties flown on 31 October, 1, 2, and 3 November 1956 – all on Canberra B.Mk 2 WD993. As usual, operational sorties were indicated in red ink, and – unlike Roy Mather – Jones named the targets for each flight, the number of bombs carried, and the altitude from which these were released. The first mission was against Almaza, the second against Cairo West, third against Luxor and the fourth against Almaza again. (via John Dillon)

puts it in context, 50 years earlier it would have been considered as a 'police operation' in part of the Empire.

While there were a number of challenges facing those who had to plan and mount the bombing phase of Musketeer, once the crews were over the target it was the bombing technique that determined whether or not it was hit and destroyed. As we have already seen, the target marking procedure was developed only months before it was used in anger, and had to be adapted as lessons were learned during the campaign; offset marking (to avoid the obscuring of the aiming point by dust), and the use of wind-finding crews over the target to pass more accurate information to the bomb aimers, were two of the developments. However, the biggest problem was the need to drop the bombs visually from high level, a deviation from the way the crews had been trained. As has been noted, the Valiant and Canberra squadrons were normally based in Europe and the UK and trained for a European war. The Valiants were intended to drop nuclear bombs using the NBS equipment for navigation and bombing, though not all had yet been brought up to this specification. The Canberras were trained to deliver their weapons using GEE-H as the bombing aid. In a peacetime environment, bombing is normally done on a range in a controlled environment and with light practice bombs, only rarely were live 1,000lb bombs used. The author only dropped 1,000lb bombs on two range sorties in five years on the Vulcan, at other times 25lb practice bombs were carried. This difference was cited in the ATFC report as one contributory factor in the disappointing results:

> Lack of practice by crews in bombing with a full load. The handling characteristics of a heavily laden aircraft on a bombing run are markedly worse than with only a light load of practice bombs.[9]

Perhaps the biggest factor was the lack of practice in visual bombing, as the same report made clear:

> For many years the primary bombing method of the Canberra force has been Gee H. In recent months, however, the emphasis was placed on visual bombing in preparation for 'Musketeer' and a directive to this effect was issued by Headquarters Bomber Command. Nevertheless, in spite of this directive, discussions with the Bomber Wings have revealed that a number of crews

Valiant B.Mk 1 WZ399 of No. 549 Squadron, seen at RAF Luqa in November 1956. The jet flew no combat sorties during the Suez War, but visible in the rear is one of Canberra PR.Mk 7s from No. 59 Squadron that did: aircraft of that unit were recognisable by their crudely applied 'Suez Stripes'. (Albert Grandolini Collection)

had not had any practice in visual bombing. This is a grave reflection on the preparation of squadrons for this operation.

How often in military history do we read of senior commanders, issuing orders and directives, with no follow-up to see if they have been implemented? – the Star Trek approach, "Make it so!"

In early January 1957, the Under Secretary of State for Air (Christopher Soames) made a visit to some of the returned crews at RAF Binbrook. This may well have been the usual goodwill visit that politicians like to make to service personnel during, and on conclusion, of military operations. Unfortunately, some of Soames' questioning of the Canberra crews laid open the issue of visual bombing training, as he made clear to the Vice-Chief of the Air Staff and the Secretary of State for Air: "I was rather disturbed to hear that the majority of them were bombing visually on target indicators for the first time as they had had no training in this technique."[10]

Soames was told that the Canberra force concentrated on bombing with GEE-H, rather than visual bombing and he wondered if that was wise 'in view of the importance which we must attach to limited war capability'. Given the build-up in the V-Force, the political importance of the Grapple nuclear bomb tests and the Cold War environment in the 1950s and 1960s, it would not be surprising if the RAF had little concentration on 'limited war'. Soames reinforced his point with a reference to the comments of crews on the raid against Cairo Radio:

> I asked why the attack on Cairo Radio had been comparatively unsuccessful. I was told that the crews were briefed to carry out this attack at 3,000 feet, which, at the speed they were travelling, made it extremely difficult to be accurate. Could this be a pointer to the need for more visual bombing training?

In the draft of his reply to the Chief of the Air Staff (CAS),[11] the VCAS recognised the comments as 'fair' but set out some of the reasons for the poor results. He acknowledged that the Air Staff had given priority to Bomber Command's training for the global war task, in particular on the primary role of the Canberra force in support of SACEUR [Supreme Allied Command Europe]'. The weather in the UK, together with the Canberra's tail actuator problem (we saw one of the crews experience this on Musketeer), had limited the opportunities for visual bombing. During their normal training (BTRs have been mentioned in a previous chapter), the crews were expected to do three visual bomb attacks for every five using GEE-H, but the weather and serviceability problems had reduced this to three in 10. The VCAS made the point that bombing on Target Indicators should not have been a problem as these are easier to identify than 'the normal visual target'. However, the note that all the crews on Musketeer 'had carried out at least one bombing exercise using target indicators' did not smack of rigorous pre-operation training. As regards Cairo Radio, the VCAS made the point that, if it could have been arranged 'it would have been a better target for ground attack aircraft'.

IN SUMMARY

The crews and technicians deployed to Malta and Cyprus performed well, given the operational limitations they had to contend with: navigation and bombing aids were limited; political interference restricted the necessary photographic reconnaissance; senior commanders were in the dark regarding the role of Israel; the Canberras were at the limit of their range when operating from Malta and the whole force had to employ Second World War bombing techniques. The aim of neutralising the EAF was quickly achieved, but only because of good weather in theatre and the very limited opposition put up by the Egyptians. The picture may have looked very different had there been a more determined opponent. The report by the Air Task Force Headquarters, written after the conclusion of Musketeer alluded to this point:

> [O]nly in a few instances were runways put out of action [...] the subsequent attacks by allied ground attack aircraft were virtually unopposed. Furthermore, reconnaissance suggests that for several days no attempts were made to recuperate from these attacks or even take steps to guard against repeat attacks.[12]

In the years following Musketeer, up and till Polaris took over the mantle of Britain's nuclear deterrent, Bomber Command continued to train to drop conventional iron bombs, but the RAF's main role was the nuclear support of SACEUR. The Canberra force, before being superseded by the Phantom, Buccaneer and Tornado, developed a technique for low level bombing using the American LABS equipment, while the V-Force moved completely away from visual bombing in favour of their NBS, which was developed for both high and low level attacks.

The events of Suez in 1956 do not rank as a high point in British diplomacy, but the RAF crews involved in Musketeer cannot be held accountable for that. Deployed to the Mediterranean the crews, technicians and administrative staff involved in the operation performed the task they were given, with the tools available to them. If the bombing results fell short of those expected by senior staff headquarters, then those officers should look to their role in designing and enforcing the training regimes that prepared the crews for this limited war outside the European theatre.

BIBLIOGRAPHY

BOOKS

Aloni, S., *Israeli Air Force Operations in the 1956 Suez War* (Solihull: Helion & Co., 2015)

Barker, A.J., *Suez: The Seven Day War* (London: Faber and Faber, 1964)

Barr, J., *Lords of the Desert. Britain's Struggle with America to Dominate the Middle East* (London: Simon & Schuster, 2018)

Blackman, T. and Wright, A., *Valiant Boys* (London: Grub Street, 2014)

Cooper, T., Nicolle, Dr. D., *MiGs in the Middle East, Volume 2: Soviet-Designed Combat Aircraft in Egypt and Syria, 1963-1966* (Warwick: Helion & Co. 2021)

Cull, B. & Nicolle, D, with Aloni, S., *Wings Over Suez* (London: Grub Street, 2006)

Downey, B., *V Bombers* (London: Arms and Armour Press, 1985)

Fursenko, A, and Naftali, T., *Khrushchev's Cold War. The Inside Story of an American Adversary* (London: W.W. Norton, 2006)

Hubbard, K., and Simmons, M., *Dropping Britain's First H-Bomb. The Story of Operation Grapple 1957/58* (Barnsley: Pen & Sword, 2008)

Kyle, K., *Suez* (London: Weidenfeld and Nicolson, 1991)

Nicolle, Dr. D., Cooper, T., *MiGs in the Middle East, Volume 1: Soviet-Designed Combat Aircraft in Egypt, Iraq & Syria, 1955-1963* (Warwick: Helion & Co., 2021)

Nicolle, Dr. D., Gabr, Air Vice Marshal Gabr Ali, Cooper, T., *Wings over Sinai: The Egyptian Air Force during the Sinai War, 1956* (Solihull: Helion & Co., 2017)

Thorpe, D.R., *Eden. The life and times of Anthony Eden First Earl of Avon, 1897-1977* (London: Chatto & Windus, 2003)

ARTICLES

Feast, S., 'War Ops: Suez. How Al Greethurst's bombing and navigation skills in the English Canberra were tested during the Suez Crisis', *FlyPast*, June 2019, pp.46-51.

Jones, F.H., 'On being a Canberra pilot on No. 44 (Rhodesia) Squadron during Operation

Musketeer (Suez Crisis)', *No. 44 (Rhodesia) Squadron Association Newsletter*, Spring 2020, pp.6-14.

Kyle, K., 'Setting the Scene' from 'A Seminar on the Air Aspects of the Suez Campaign – 1956',

Royal Air Force Historical Society Journal, Vol. 3, 1988, pp.10-15.

Lee, D., 'The View from Whitehall', *Royal Air Force Historical Society Journal*, Vol.3, 1988, pp.16-18.

Mallorie, P., 'Suez – A Squadron Commander's Viewpoint', *Royal Air Force Historical Society*

Journal, Vol. 43a, 2008, pp.116-120.

Paton, D., 'Airborne electronic reconnaissance, 1948 to 1989', *Royal Air Force Historical Society*

Journal, Vol. 23, 2000, pp.59-68.

Smallwood, D., 'The planners' perspective', *Royal Air Force Historical Society Journal*. Vol.3. pp.26-34.

PHD THESIS;

Al-Solami, D., 'British Preparations for the Suez War – 1956', Exeter University, 1988.

ONLINE RESOURCES

Goodall, P., 'Over fifty years ago I bombed Egypt', www.vforcereunion.co.uk/article7.html, (last accessed 23 September 2020).

Mather, R., 'A Pilot's Story', www.vickersvaliant.com, (last accessed 23 September 2020).

NOTES

CHAPTER 1

1 A. Tunzelmann, *Blood and Sand. Suez, Hungary and the crisis that shook the world* (London: Simon & Schuster, 2016), p.5.
2 Tunzelmann, *Blood and Sand*, p.8.
3 Tunzelmann, *Blood and Sand*, p.10.
4 D. Al-Solami, 'British Preparations for the Suez War – 1956', unpublished PhD thesis, Exeter University, September 1988.
5 Tunzelmann, *Blood and Sand*, p.115.

CHAPTER 2

1 TNA CAB 195/15/18, Cabinet minutes, 27 July 1956.
2 K. Kyle, *Royal Air Force Historical Society Journal*, No.3, January 1988, p.10.
3 D.R. Thorpe, *Eden. The life and times of Anthony Eden First Earl of Avon, 1897-1977* (London: Chatto & Windus, 2003), p.482.
4 TNA, CAB 195/15/18.
5 TNA, AIR 20/10601, memo regarding forces available for operations in M.E.A.F.
6 Tunzelmann, *Blood and Sand*, p.220.
7 Thorpe, *Eden*, p.519.
8 Tunzelmann, *Blood and Sand*, p.114.

CHAPTER 3

1 TNA, AIR 14/4013.
2 Kyle, *RAFHSJ*, No.3, p.14.
3 Cooper, *RAFHSJ*, No.3, pp.21-23.
4 Smallwood, *RAFHSJ*, No.3, p.26.
5 Lee, *RAFHSJ*, No.3, p.16.
6 TNA, AIR 20/10746, ATFC report, p.2.
7 TNA, AIR 20/10746, ATFC report, p.3.
8 TNA, AIR 20/10601, report by Joint Planning Staff, 1 August 1956, p.1.
9 TNA, AIR 20/10746
10 TNA, AIR 20/10746, ATFC report, p.4.

CHAPTER 4

1 For details on allied air power, see Cull et all, *Wings over Suez*; for details on the Israeli Air Force during the Suez War of 1956, see Aloni, *Israeli Air Fore Operations in the 1956 Suez War*; for details on the Egyptian Air Force, see Nicolle et all, *Wings over Sinai* and Nicolle et all, *MiGs in the Middle East, Volume 1*.
2 TNA, AIR 20/10601, signal 30 July 1956.
3 TNA, AIR 20/10746.
4 TNA, AIR 20/10601, signal, 30 July 1956.
5 TNA, AIR 20/10601, memo from ACAS, 3 August 1956.
6 TNA, CAB 128/30/57.
7 TNA, CAB 128/30/72.
8 TNA, AIR 8/2111, handwritten note of aircraft types, their operational loads and combat radius.
9 Thomas, A., 'Canberra sub-types guide'. *Flypast*, June 2019, p.52.
10 TNA, AIR 8/2111, map of area with distances from British bases to Cairo.
11 TNA, AIR 8/2111, handwritten note of aircraft types, their operational loads and combat radius.
12 TNA, AIR 20/10601, memo on Forces available for Operations in M.E.A.F.
13 TNA, AIR 20/10601, memo on deployment of 1,000lb H.E. bombs, 2 August 1956.
14 TNA, AIR 20/10601, signal 1138 from ACAS to AOC in Malta, 31 July 1956.
15 Jones, F.H., 'On being a Canberra pilot on No. 44 (Rhodesia) Squadron during Operation Musketeer (Suez Crisis)', No. 44 (Rhodesia) Squadron Association Newsletter, Spring 2020, p.6.
16 TNA, AIR 20/10601, memo 31 July 1956.
17 TNA, AIR 20/10601, planning document, 3 August 1956.

CHAPTER 5

1 TNA, AIR 14/4013, minutes of a conference, 3 November 1954, p.5.
2 Telephone conversation between the author and George Perrin, 24 April 2020.
3 TNA, AVIA 6/19056, High altitude bombing trial with the prototype T-4 bombsight.
4 TNA, AVIA 6/19056, bombing trial report, appendix II, Figure 1.
5 TNA, AIR 27/2818, Operation Order, 14 February 1956, p.2.
6 More detail on G-H can be obtained by making an internet search for 'GEE Hyperbolic Navigation System'. Thanks to Roger Green for making me aware of this site.
7 Report on Blue Shadow development supplied to the author by John King who flew with 139 Squadron prior to Suez.
8 Report from John King.
9 TNA, AIR 27/2818, report on target illumination and marking trials, 7 April 1956, p.3.
10 Telephone conversation between the author and George Perrin, 24 April 2020.
11 T. Blackman and A. Wright, *Valiant Boys* (London: Grub Street, 2006), p.47.
12 Blackman and Wright, *Valiant Boys*, p.36.
13 TNA, AIR 20/10746, Bombing technique on target indicators, 28 October 1956.
14 TNA, AIR 20/10746, Memo on Revised Marking Procedure, 11 November 1956.
15 Meteorological officer.
16 In this context a "stick" is a group of bombs released nearly-simultaneously from one aircraft.

CHAPTER 6

1 TNA, AIR 20/10601, signal from CAS, 1088, 30 July 1956, p.2.
2 TNA, AIR 20/10601, signal from C-in-C, 31 July 1956.
3 TNA, AIR 8/2088, loose minute, 2 August 1956.
4 TNA, AIR 20/10601, signal A2365, 17 August 1956.
5 TNA, AIR 20/10746, Report of Air Task Force Commander, 'Events leading up to D-Day'.
6 TNA, AIR 20/10601, from CAS, Revised timings for redeployment of bomber and transport forces, 29 August 1956.
7 TNA, AIR 8/2111, Dates of despatch of bomber forces, and Cull, *Wings over Suez*, pp.164-165.
8 Jones, *Personal account*, p.6.
9 TNA, AIR 27/2756/17.
10 Jones, *Personal account*, p.7.
11 TNA, AIR 27/2730/41.
12 TNA, AIR 27/2807/45, 101 Squadron ORB.
13 TNA, AIR 20/10746, annex G, 11 November 1956.
14 Goodall, P., *Over fifty years ago I bombed Egypt*, www.vforcereunion.co.uk/article7.html.
15 TNA, AIR 20/10746, ATFC report, p.3.
16 TNA, AIR 20/10746, ATFC report, p.3.

17 TNA, AIR 2/12507, Alacrity conference, 19 July 1954, p.5.
18 TNA, AIR 20/10746, annex 'D' to Air Plan.
19 TNA, AIR 20/10746, Annex 'D', Rates of Effort.
20 TNA, AIR 24/2426, HQ Air Task Force.
21 Smallwood, *RAFHSJ*, No.3, p.30.
22 TNA, AIR 20/10363, signal from HQ Air Task Force, 30 October 1956. For actual figures, see Nicolle et all, *Wings over Sinai*.
23 TNA, AIR 8/2111, signal from Keightley to Ministry of Defence, 30 October 1956.

CHAPTER 7

1 Kyle, *RAFHSJ*, No.3, p.15.
2 Tunzelmann, *Blood and Sand*, p.217.
3 Tunzelmann, *Blood and Sand*, p.228, signal to Chiefs, 31 October.
4 Kyle, *Suez*, p.410.
5 Tunzelmann, *Blood and Sand*, p.210.
6 TNA, CAB 128/30/76, minutes of Cabinet meeting, 12.30 p.m., 31 October 1956.
7 TNA, AIR 20/10215, memo to Chiefs of Staff, 2 October 1956.
8 TNA, AIR 20/10746.
9 TNA, AIR 20/10746.
10 TNA, AIR 20/10746.
11 TNA, AIR 8/2111, signal (COSKEY 5) from COS to Keightley, 31 October 1956.
12 TNA, AIR 20/10746.
13 Mallorie, P., *Royal Air Force Historical Society Journal*, No.43a, April 2008, p.118.
14 Paton, D., 'Airborne electronic reconnaissance, 1948 to 1989', *Royal Air Force Historical Society Journal*, Vol. 23, 2000, p.64.
15 TNA, AIR 8/2111, signal from Barnet to Air Ministry, 30 October 1956.
16 TNA, AIR 8/2111, signal KEYCOS 11.
17 TNA, AIR 20/10746.
18 Blackman and Wright, *Valiant Boys*, p.46.
19 Jones, *Personal account*, p.7.
20 TNA, AIR 20/10746, appendix 13.
21 TNA, AIR 20/10746, appendix 13.
22 TNA, AIR 20/10746, appendix 13, p.2.
23 TNA, AIR 27/2840/17, 214 Squadron ORB.
24 B. Cull, D. Nicolle and S. Aloni, *Wings over Suez* (London: Grub Street, 2006), p.189.

CHAPTER 8

1 TNA, AIR 20/10746, ATFC report, p.5.
2 Cull, *Wings over Suez*, p.187.
3 TNA, AIR 20/10746, ATFC report, Air Directive 1/56, p.2.
4 TNA, AIR 20/10746.
5 TNA, CAB 128/30/76, minutes of Cabinet meeting, 31 October 1956.
6 TNA, AIR 8/2111, signal 1182/CAS.
7 TNA, AIR 8/2111, signal KEYCOS 4.
8 Cull, *Wings over Suez*, p.192.
9 Blackman and Wright, *Valiant Boys*, p.44.
10 As an aside, Woodroffe was killed on 9 October 1957 in an American B-47 flown by Colonel M. McCoy during a demonstration at Pinecastle Air Force Base, Florida.
11 TNA, AIR 20/10746, appendix 13 to F.540, p.4.
12 TNA, AIR 20/10746, appendix 13 to F.540, p.4.
13 P. Mallorie, *Royal Air Force Historical Society Journal*, No.43a, April 2008, p.119.
14 TNA, AIR 20/10746, appendix 13 to F.540, p.3.
15 Jones, *Personal account*, p.8.
16 TNA, AIR 27/2818, pp.232-233.
17 TNA, AIR 27/2818, p.232/2.
18 Jones, *Personal account*, p.8.
19 TNA, AIR 27/2775/17, 44 Squadron ORB.
20 TNA, AIR 27/2818, raid report, p.232.
21 Jones, *Personal account*, p.9.
22 The author was a Navigator Radar on Vulcans, which used the NBS/H2S system.
23 TNA, AIR 27/2691/44.
24 TNA, AIR 27/2810/48.
25 S. Feast, 'War Ops: Suez. How Al Greethurst's bombing and navigation skills in the English Electric Canberra were tested during the Suez Crisis'. *Flypast*, June 2019, p.49.
26 TNA, AIR 27/2828, p.233.
27 Cull, *Wings over Suez*, p.193.
28 TNA, AIR 27/2828, p.233.
29 Cull, *Wings over Suez*, p.193.
30 TNA, AIR 27/2821/7.
31 TNA, AIR 27/2821/7.
32 Cull, *Wings over Suez*, p.193.
33 Feast, *Greethurst's article*, pp.49-50.
34 TNA, AIR 27/2810/47.
35 Kyle, *Suez*, p.383.
36 TNA, AIR 20/10746, appendix 13, para. 20.
37 TNA, AIR 27/2818, p.232.
38 TNA, AIR 27/2818, p.233.
39 TNA, AIR 20/10746.
40 TNA, AIR 27/2835/10.
41 TNA, AIR 27/2807/46.
42 TNA, AIR 27/2807/45.
43 TNA, AIR 27/2840/17.
44 Blackman and Wright, *Valiant Boys*, p.48.
45 TNA, AIR 27/2815/16.
46 Jones, *Personal account*, p.11.
47 TNA, AIR 20/10746, Annex 'D'.
48 Cull, *Wings over Suez*, p.190.
49 TNA, AIR 27/2807/45.
50 Kyle, *Suez*, pp.384-385.
51 TNA, AIR 27/2756/20.
52 TNA, AIR 27/2756/19.
53 TNA, AIR 27/2818, Kearns report, p.234.

CHAPTER 9

1 Jones, *Personal account*, p.7.

CHAPTER 10

1 Jones, *Personal account*, p.10.
2 TNA, AIR 27/2818, Slater's report, p.235.
3 TNA, AIR 27/2818, Slater's report, p.235.
4 Blackman and Wright, *Valiant Boys*, p.45.
5 Jones, *Personal account*, p.10.
6 TNA, AIR 27/2818, p.236.
7 TNA, AIR 27/2744/20, 27 Squadron ORB. The author has dropped 1,000lb bombs from a Vulcan but has no further explanation of this fault.
8 TNA, AIR 27/2818, p.236.
9 TNA, AIR 27/2736/17.
10 TNA, AIR 27/2821/9, 148 Squadron ORB.
11 TNA, AIR 27/2810/48.
12 TNA, AIR 27/2730/46.

CHAPTER 11

1 TNA, AIR 20/10746, ATFC report, p.5.
2 TNA, AIR 20/10746, ATFC report, p.6.
3 TNA, AIR 20/10746, signal AO 476.
4 TNA, AIR 20/10746, ATFC report, p.5.
5 TNA, AIR 8/2111, memo from VCAS to Under Secretary of State, 31 January 1957.
6 TNA, AIR 20/10363, signal AG 627, INTOPSUM 9.
7 TNA, AIR 8/2111.
8 TNA, AIR 20/10746, Annex 'D', p.2.
9 Cull, *Wings over Suez*, p.238.
10 TNA, AIR 27/2775/17.
11 TNA, AIR 20/10746.
12 Jones, *Personal account*, pp.10-11.
13 TNA, AIR 27/2736/17.
14 TNA, AIR 20/10363, signal AG 627 INTOPSUM 9.
15 TNA, AIR 27/2818, Mallorie's report, p.237.
16 TNA, AIR 27/2818, Mallorie's report, p.237, para.5.
17 TNA, AIR 20/10746, ATFC report.
18 TNA, AIR 27/2744/20.
19 TNA, AIR 20/10746, appendix 13 to Air Staff F.540, p.5.
20 Cull, *Wings over Suez*, pp.262-263.
21 TNA, AIR 27/2815/20.
22 Blackman and Wright, *Valiant Boys*, p.45.
23 Blackman and Wright, *Valiant Boys*, p.45.
24 TNA, AIR 27/2818, pp.239-240.
25 Cull, *Wings over Suez*, p.264.
26 TNA, AIR 20/10746, annex 'D', p.2.
27 Feast, *Greethurst's article*, p.51.

CHAPTER 12

1 Cull, *Wings over Suez*, p.264.
2 TNA, AIR 27/2817/22.
3 TNA, AIR 27/2692/76.
4 TNA, AIR 20/10746, appendix 13, p.5.
5 TNA, AIR 20/10746, signal AG 631 INTOPSUM 10.
6 TNA, AIR 20/10746, annex 'D', p.3.
7 TNA, AIR 27/2744/20.
8 TNA, AIR 20/10746, appendix 13, p.5.
9 TNA, AIR 20/10746, appendix 13, p.6.
10 TNA, AIR 27/2840/18.
11 TNA, AIR 20/10746, ATFC report, p.6.
12 TNA, AIR 20/10746, appendix 13, p.5.
13 TNA, AIR 27/2828, p.241.
14 TNA, AIR 27/2810/48.
15 Email from R. Ellicott to H. Jones, forwarded to the author, 17 April 2020.
16 TNA, AIR 27/2807/46.

CHAPTER 13

1 Tunzelmann, *Blood and Sand*, p.319.
2 TNA, AIR 27/2828, p.243.
3 TNA, AIR 20/10746, annex 'D', p.3.
4 One suggestion is A.J.Barker, *Suez: The Seven Day War* (London: Faber and Faber, 1964).
5 TNA, AIR 20/10746, ATFC report, p.3.
6 TNA, AIR 27/2818, p.244.
7 Jones, *Personal account*, pp.12-13.

CHAPTER 14

1 TNA, AIR 20/10746, AFTC report, p.7.
2 TNA, AIR 20/10746, appendix 13, p.6.
3 TNA, AIR 27/1744/21.
4 Blackman and Wright, *Valiant Boys*, p.48.
5 TNA, CAB 128/30/79, minutes of meeting, 6.30pm, 4 November.
6 TNA, CAB 128/30/80, minutes of meeting, 9.45am, 6 November.
7 TNA, CAB 128/30/82, minutes of meeting, 11.15am, 8 November.
8 TNA, CAB 128/30/82, minutes of meeting, 11.15am, 8 November, p.2, para (b).
9 Fursenko, A., and T. Naftali, *Khrushchev's Cold War. The inside story of an American adversary* (London: W.W. Norton, 2006), p.137.
10 TNA, AIR 8/2111, signal 1674/A.C.A.S. (OPS), 061700Z.
11 TNA, AIR 8/2111, signal KEYCOS/46, 061814Z.
12 Jones, *Personal account*, p.13.
13 TNA, AIR 27/2744/22.
14 TNA, AIR 8/2111, signal 1805/D.D.OPS., 071705Z.

CHAPTER 15

1 TNA, AIR 8/2111, report by D.D.Ops. (TAC.)/TS.301/III, 19 February 1957, p.9.
2 TNA, AIR 20/10746, ATFC report, p.2.
3 Tunzelmann, Blood and Sand, p.303.
4 Mallorie, Royal Air Force Historical Society Journal, No.43a, p.120.
5 TNA, AIR 27/2818, p.226.
6 TNA, AIR 27/2818, p.228.
7 TNA, AIR 20/10746, ATFC report, appendix 'D', 27 November 1956, p.2.
8 TNA, AIR 20/10746, appendix 13, p.7.
9 TNA, AIR 20/10746, appendix 13, p.7.
10 TNA, AIR 8/2111, memo from USoS to VCAS, LM 9857, 9 January 1957.
11 TNA, AIR 8/2111, memo from VCAS to CAS, 24 January 1957.
12 TNA, AIR 20/10746, appendix 13, p.7, 11 November 1956.

ABOUT THE AUTHOR

John Dillon joined the RAF in 1963 as an apprentice followed by three years as an officer cadet at Cranwell and six years as a navigator on Vulcan bombers. He left the service in 1976 for a career in mainframe computers. In 2005 he went to Reading University as a mature student, studying history for a PhD.

His previous books (with Helion) are *'Allies are a Tiresome Lot' The British Army in Italy in the First World War* followed by *Battalions at War: The York and Lancaster Regiment in the First World War* and *All at Sea. Naval support for the British Army during the American Revolutionary War.*

John and his wife live in Berkshire.